66 ...although it was June, the immense body of snow baffled all our exertions, and we were compelled to content ourselves with listening to marvelous tales of burning plains, immense lakes, and boiling springs, without being able to verify these wonders. **99**

Captain W. F. Raynolds
1860

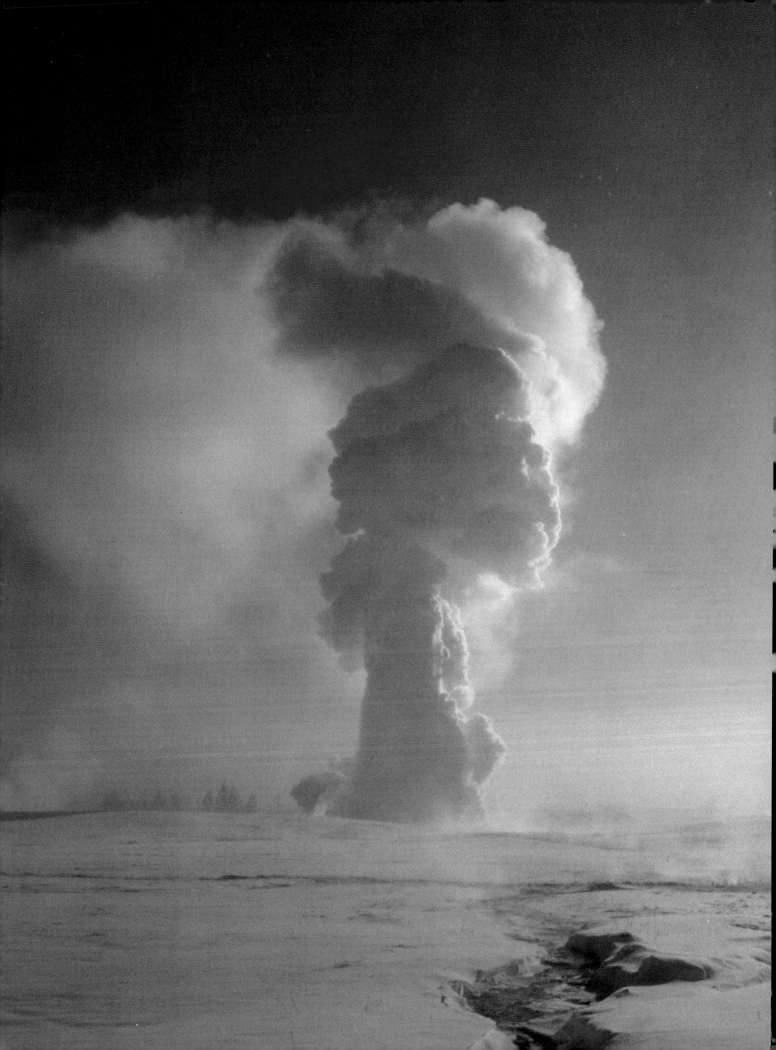

66 I think a more confirmed set of skeptics never went out into the wilderness than those who composed our party, and never was a party more completely surprised and captivated with the wonders of nature. **99**

Cornelius Hedges
1870

66 The intelligent American will one day point on the map to this remarkable district with the conscious pride that it has not its parallel on the face of the globe. 99

Ferdinand V. Hayden
1872

66 Indeed, it is quite impossible for any one to do justice to the remarkable physical phenomena of this valley by any description, however vivid. It is only through the eye that the mind can form anything like an adequate conception of their beauty and grandeur. **99**

Ferdinand V. Hayden
1872

Yellowstone

Photographs
and
Text
by
Fred Hirschmann

Graphic
Arts
Center
Publishing
Company

Portland,
Oregon

International Standard Book Number 0-912856-75-0
Library of Congress Number 81-86038

Designer: Joseph Erceg
Typesetting: Paul O. Giesey/Adcrafters
Printing: Bridgetown
Binding: Lincoln & Allen

Printed in the United States of America

Revised 1990
Third Printing

Night photograph of
Yellowstone Fire
by Jennifer Whipple

Table of
Contents

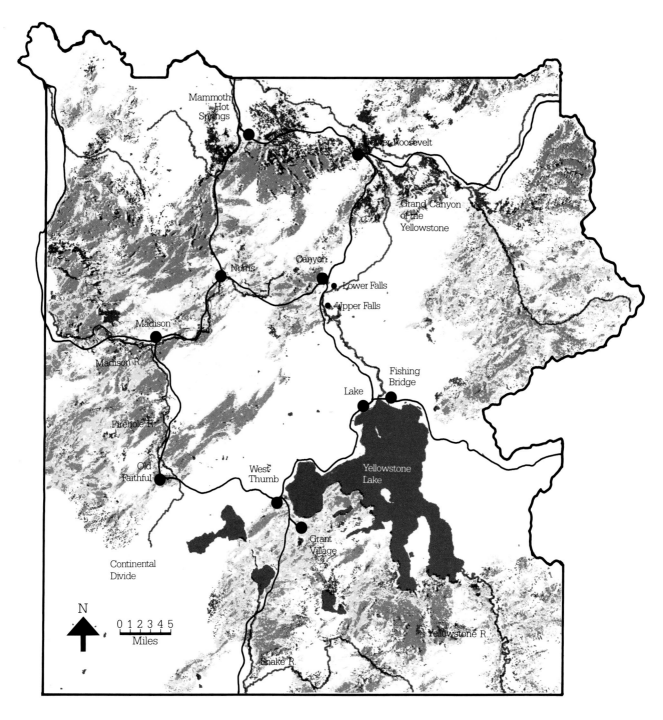

Areas impacted by 1988 fires.

Canopy Burn

Mixed Burn

Nonforested Burn

Undifferentiated Burn

Water

— Roads

" After weeks of continual new
discoveries, becoming more and more
wonderful till wonder itself became
paralyzed, I am satisfied that we saw
but a fraction of the strange sights the
country contains.**"**

Cornelius Hedges
1870

Yellowstone. Say the name and nearly everyone has a vision. It evokes images of hundreds of hot springs and geysers, the massive Grand Canyon of the Yellowstone, and the spectacular fires of 1988. One also imagines great herds of wild elk and bison, snowcapped peaks, and crystalline lakes preserved in almost the same condition as when the first mountain men gazed upon the Rockies. In addition, Yellowstone represents a philosophy that has traveled around the world. The National Park Idea calls for keeping portions of Earth natural, where humans only observe and do not interfere.

Yet pleasant memories of Yellowstone's grandeur often are mixed with recollections of huge summer crowds. Elk jams, moose jams, bison jams, even ranger jams delay motorists. During busy summers, campgrounds fill by 9:30 a.m. Families race across the park at sunrise searching for another campsite. When they observe the spectacle of Old Faithful, they may find its drama diminished by the sounds of clicking camera shutters and noisy exclamations from the crowd drowning the roar of a 130-foot eruption.

The Yellowstone visitor is caught between appreciating the world's crown jewel of national parks and sharing that experience with 30,000 others on a busy summer day. The multitudes seeking Yellowstone's splendor, however, can find enjoyment by slowing down and taking a closer look at the park. More than 1,000 miles of backcountry trails await them.

A few years ago, I accompanied Park Geologist Rick Hutchinson on an expedition to inventory hot spring activity below the Madison Plateau in the southwest corner of the park. Topographic maps did not show the presence of hot springs. Similarity to areas of known geothermal activity indicated a strong likelihood of thermal features.

We hiked north beyond 250-foot Silver Scarf Falls, whose ribbon of shimmering water may be the world's highest thermal cascade. Nearby, graceful Dunanda Falls plummeted 150 feet. At its base, known hot spring fed pools offered sharp contrast to the cool waterfall spray.

Above Dunanda, subtle clues suggested we would soon find additional hot spring activity. The creek supplying Dunanda Falls lacked the icy snap of water from Yellowstone's cold water springs that average a chilly 39°F. Luxuriant green algae growth appeared nurtured by warm water.

Continuing upstream, clues became more pronounced. The creek water definitely was warming. Protruding cobbles carried white incrustations of siliceous sinter, a mineral often deposited by cooling thermal waters.

We left the main creek to explore many dry washes traversing westward off the plateau. Elephant-sized boulders were scattered through dried gullies.

Steam gently rose from many gully bottoms in the cool October afternoon air. Hot (175°F) water gushed from cracks in the flood-scoured gulches. We counted forty hot springs and seeps in twenty-six acres of gullies and boulder strewn slopes. This was Yellowstone's 103rd thermal area to be inventoried.

Following hot rivulets back to the main creek, we found evidence of additional thermal activity farther upstream. Hiking a mile north, the creek warmed to comfortable bath temperature.

Yellowstone's geyser basins exhibit a palette of vibrant colors. The setting sun illuminates the shallow terraced pools of a peaceful Ledge Geyser at Norris (below). During its infrequent eruptions, Ledge shoots an angled column of boiling water up to 180 feet away from its vent. Hidden in the backcountry near an unnamed lake is a seething red cauldron (right), colored by iron oxides.

Excitement overcame our scientific curiosity. Our minds returned to 1870 when the Washburn, Langford, and Doane expedition circumambulated the land that became Yellowstone National Park. Their diaries glow as they describe "the greatest wonders on the continent." We, too, were caught in the joy of discovery. Our talk became boastful joking. We speculated that by rounding the next bend we would find a sparkling pool that would suddenly burst forth with terrific force and send a boiling water column 150 feet into the air.

Past the next curve, we stopped abruptly. The vista terminated in not one

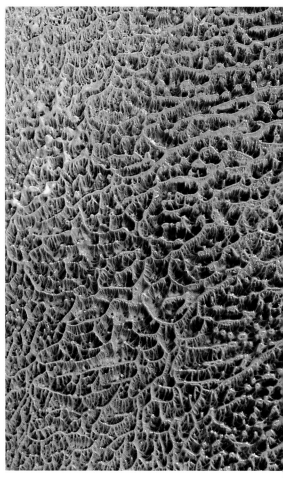

An infinite variety of patterns are created by thermal water. At Mammoth Hot Springs (left), travertine, a calcium carbonate mineral, builds terraces of unsurpassed beauty. More than a foot of travertine may be added each year. Thermophilic life often aids hot spring formation growth. Certain species of algae and bacteria incorporate silicon dioxide from geyser water. These organisms weave an intricate pattern in Goggle Geyser's runoff (above).

but two towering white columns. We hurriedly crossed the distance between us and the emerging stream. Not geysers but two growling fumaroles were ejecting superheated water vapor. Scattered around the two steam vents were numerous springs sizzling like water drops on a hot frying pan. Gray mud pots with black pyrite film, sulfurous springs, and many smaller fumaroles joined the activity in this little basin.

About 800 feet farther along the river was a second smaller basin. Among its collection of frying pan springs and assorted pots was a jumble of rocks laying over a fissure. Peering into the crack, we could see only inky blackness. Downhill from the fissure in the soft ground and decomposing rhyolite volcanic rock loomed a freshly eroded square-walled gully. Lodgepole pines near the crevice were dying. Muddy gray silt coated their needles. The deep run-off channel and silt coated trees were indisputable evidence that this was the geyser that less than an hour before had been the object of our explorer's dreams.

We unfortunately did not see the geyser erupt. On the last day of sampling, however, water gurgled deep within its vent. Although 1,000 names already identify Yellowstone's thermal features, we decided to leave this new geyser unnamed. Perhaps without a name, the next person who stumbles across this spouter will feel closer to its discovery.

Certainly others had seen the three thermal basins we inventoried. During the 1930s, trail cutting crews of the Civilian Conservation Corps surely gazed into the steaming holes. In subsequent years, backcountry park rangers must have as well. Yet 107 years following the park's discovery passed before descriptions of these three areas entered park annals.

Across Yellowstone's 3,472 square miles, many secrets remain. From the most remote backcountry sections come tales of unnamed waterfalls plummeting 200 feet, rivers whose water is too hot to touch, oil-coated hot springs shimmering with irridescent colors, and a forest of extinct hot spring cones towering above the ground. Perhaps these modern day stories are nothing more than the mountain man yarns of one and a half centuries ago. Yet we now know that Jim Bridger's tales about mountains of glass, petrified forests, and rivers that cooked fish were based upon truths.

Visitors need not journey into Yellowstone's wildlands to take part in discovery. The major geyser basins visited by the Grand Loop Road constantly change. Almost every year, at least one new geyser emerges.

Occasionally the new feature takes off in glorious style. On February 14, 1902, C. W. Bronson, the winter keeper employed to shovel snow off the roof of the then existing Norris Hotel, watched the birth of Valentine Geyser. The winter peace of Norris was shattered. Quantities of rock, mud, water, and steam were disgorged as the geyser played two hours to a height of 225 feet. Valentine Geyser still erupts, but not to such extremes.

On the park's fiftieth anniversary in 1922, Semi-Centennial Geyser made its grand entry. A pool occupying a placid stretch of Obsidian Creek suddenly sent explosions of muddy water 300 feet into the air. Huge amounts of hot water destroyed the surrounding forest before Semi-Centennial Geyser slumped into a dormancy, continuing to the present.

Even if you do not view events like Semi-Centennial, Yellowstone offers countless opportunities for small personal discoveries. For those willing to crawl on hands and knees, a Lilliputian world awaits. Most park hot springs support extensive beds of algae and bacteria. Ephydra or brine flies live year-round on the warm algae. A close observer can watch the flies feed, mate, lay eggs, become infested with tiny red mites, or be gobbled by killdeers and ravens.

If one is patient, it is possible to watch the flies scuba dive. One wintry afternoon I spied an ephydra fly feeding on a portion of an algal mat sloping beneath the water surface. As the fly descended, the water dimpled; the surface tension became too weak to support the fly in an airborne world. The depression broke suddenly, and warm water swallowed the tiny insect. I assumed I had witnessed a drowning, but to my amazement the fly continued feeding. On its back was a silver dome of air left by the departing dimple. Possibly the air bubble insulated the fly or provided a portable oxygen supply. After feeding, the fly could release its grip from the algae and balloon back to the surface.

Visitors to Yellowstone can leave the crowds and quietly learn about the wonders of nature. By observing and listening, they can view the Earth's mysteries; and in this learning and discovery are some of Yellowstone's finest pleasures.

66 Suddenly, and while we were
returning to camp,—with a tremendous
spasm, which threatened to tear the
very earth asunder, it threw an immense
column to the height of
two hundred feet or more.
Our party could not repress a loud
shout, and this, followed by a second eruption
of the same geyser, more wonderful, and
longer duration than the first...99

Nathaniel P. Langford
1873

June 18, 1979 was a perfect day to finish the summer woodpile. All afternoon thick wet snowflakes plopped across the Norris Geyser Basin, mocking the summer solstice just three days away. Only a handful of visitors explored the Norris trails. What better way to warm the body than by splitting wood? The cadence of my axe cleaving lodgepole logs resounded through the forest. Peace enveloped me, and I daydreamed as the woodpile grew.

Suddenly the spell was shattered. With a heavy down swing, the axe bit deeply into soft wood. Leaving the tool in place, I stepped back puzzled by a metamorphosis in the forest's mood. The woods reverberated with a deep gushing sound from the west. I was accustomed to hearing Africa Geyser's periodic sputtering drift from the geyser basin, but this low-pitched rumbling was much more intense. In a few seconds, I realized that Steamboat Geyser, the world's largest active spouter, suddenly had come to sonorous life.

At the same time a mile away, Tom Pittenger, a naturalist with nine seasons of service, was standing on the trail less than 100 feet from Steamboat's ragged gaping vent. With Tom were two visitors who had ignored the snowy June weather and joined the Park Service's afternoon guided walk. Tom told the couple tantalizing tales about Steamboat's history. He mentioned this unpredictable geyser could send immense volumes of muddy water and rocks 300 to 400 feet skyward. He pointed out skeletons of fifty-year-old lodgepole pines snapped in two by tremendous ice loads they bore following earlier winter eruptions. The visitors asked if he had witnessed a major eruption; he replied no. This was Tom's last summer at Norris. He hoped Steamboat would give him a proper goodbye.

The three walked down the boardwalk toward Echinus Geyser. When they crossed Steamboat's two gully-like runoff channels, a massive splash shot eighty feet high. Unlike Steamboat's teasing activity of previous weeks, this splash did not subside. Instead, additional water surged from below. One of the visitors nervously remarked, "Perhaps it's going to go...". Immediately following her comment, Steamboat erupted.

Tom rushed the couple to the lower viewing platform. Muddy water hurled more than 200 feet into chilly air. Sound pressure waves broke against their bodies. According to one of the visitors, "When Steamboat took off, the ranger took off! He ran up the boardwalk waving his hat, and shouting, 'It did it!'" Tom denies the performance, but who could fault him? Nine years of following Norris's trails was a long time to wait for Yellowstone National Park's grandest performer.

When I discovered that Steamboat was erupting, I quickly left my pile of lodgepole logs. When I reached the parking lot 1,000 feet north of Steamboat, a heavy spray containing fine silica granules drenched me. Far above the trees a massive fan-shaped water column blended into gray clouds and falling snow.

I rushed to the closest viewing point and watched the last few minutes of Steamboat's water phase. Even shouting my loudest, words were lost in a few feet. My body and the boardwalk on which I stood reverberated from sound pressure waves. Contrasting with the white backdrop, myriad rocks sailed 200 to 300 feet high. After the eruption, I found a softball-sized rock cradled in

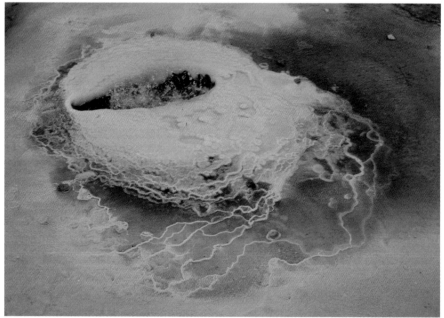

the branches of a lodgepole pine 100 feet east of Steamboat's vent.

Less than ten minutes after the initial surge, the torrent lessened. It was replaced by jets of vapor spiraling 1,000 feet. For the next forty hours, Steamboat asserted a thundering steam phase. Gradually the roar diminished, and Steamboat returned to a slumber for two and a half years, beginning a new series of eruptions on January 13, 1982.

Experiencing a Steamboat eruption

Yellowstone's hot springs exhibit wide variation in size and discharge. A small vent (below) hidden on Porcelain Terrace at Norris splashes vigorously, but produces a mere trickle of overflow. On the other hand, Minerva Spring at Mammoth (right) overflows with scores of hot rivulets building terraces of considerable grandeur. An estimated ten thousand thermal features are scattered across the more than one hundred hot spring groups within the park.

is a rare treat. Since its birth in 1878, at least 157 major eruptions have been documented. One hundred six of these displays occurred between 1961 and 1969. Another forty eruptions took place between 1982 and 1984. Steamboat Geyser has erupted as recently as October 9, 1989.

During this thermal giant's most active period, visitors stayed day and night hoping to catch a major eruption. The longest vigil was by Hazel Decker from Two Harbors, Minnesota. She waited

When Great Fountain Geyser of the Lower Geyser Basin (left) begins to erupt, people notice. Massive bursts reach 180 feet and occasionally soak spectators. Scalding water jetting from the eruption rapidly cools, enabling people watching from the road and boardwalk to experience a shower without being burned. A major spring going dormant also attracts attention. Minerva Spring's flow mysteriously ceased in 1939 and twice in 1981 (above), causing the stalactites to hang wet and dripping.

fifty-two consecutive days and nights beside Steamboat before being rewarded with an eruption. Her fondness for Steamboat was so great that she eventually saw twelve eruptions.

Intervals between major eruptions of Steamboat Geyser are often measured in years. Yellowstone has comparable outstanding geysers that have periods of inactivity lasting decades or even centuries.

The 1880s brought tremendous displays from Excelsior Geyser in the Midway Geyser Basin. Its 276 by 328-foot crater exploded in 300-foot bursts. Activity ceased in 1890. Explosions fracturing the underlying rock may have caused Excelsior's demise.

Mineral deposition, however, slowly seals heat releasing cracks over the years. Excelsior sprang back to life September 14, 1985, with 47 hours of periodic major eruptions. Presently it has the greatest steady boiling water discharge of any Yellowstone thermal feature. Every minute approximately 4,050 gallons cascade from its crater into the Firehole River.

Steamboat and Excelsior are two of Yellowstone's more than 300 geysers. Daily four to ten geysers shoot above 100 feet. Scores of smaller geysers sputter, splash, and overflow every few minutes. Their feisty displays provide considerable amusement.

The Upper Geyser Basin holds the greatest concentration of geysers. Old Faithful is the area's best known feature. Approximately every seventy-eight minutes its graceful column of water soars to 130 feet. During twenty-two hours spent exploring the Upper Geyser Basin, the 1870 Washburn expedition witnessed a dozen geysers erupting, including six features of major proportions. The explorers were enthralled with their discoveries. Nathaniel P. Langford wrote in his diary, "Judge, then, of our astonishment on entering this basin, to see at no great distance before us an immense body of sparkling water, projected suddenly and with terrific force into the air to the height of over one hundred feet. We had found a real geyser." General Washburn christened this geyser with the name "Old Faithful" because of the regularity of its eruptions. It played every sixty to sixty-five minutes during their short visit.

Old Faithful is a trustworthy performer. Since discovery, it has never missed an eruption. Intervals between crowd satisfying shows vary between thirty and one hundred twenty minutes. Old Faithful's vital statistics do not exhibit seasonal variations. The geyser's physical appearance, however, becomes stupendous during winter. Yellowstone's crystalline beauty increases as the thermometer plunges. On mornings when eyelashes freeze together, spit bounces, and snow protests every step with loud squeaks, the geyser basins become fairylands. In contrast to diminutive frost crystals coating bison, elk, and lodgepole pines, erupting geysers generate enormous billowing clouds of condensing steam.

Observing Old Faithful erupt during sunrise, when the temperature reads 50°F below zero, leaves a lasting impression. The bitter air feels motionless, yet its subtle movement wafts thousands of glistening ice prisms. Into this sequined world, rushes water 250°F hotter than the surrounding air. Old Faithful's boiling column is concealed in white robes. A mushroom shaped cloud explodes into the sky. To heights of 1,000 feet, the battle of vaporizing water hitting supercooled air makes a spectacular display.

On the sinter sheets leading from Old

23

Faithful, a second battle occurs. Warm water cascading from the geyser encounters frozen runoff from previous eruptions. Sudden warming of ice, followed by rapid freezing of newly ejected water, creates creaks, cracks, and groans, drowning Old Faithful's roar.

The tremendous release of heat so apparent during Old Faithful's winter eruptions is a minute expression of Yellowstone's total heat flow. Nineteen tons of ice could be melted every second by heat rising from beneath the park. Old Faithful's contribution of 3,500 to 8,000 gallons of boiling water during each eruption is approximately 1/1,000th of Yellowstone's total thermal output.

Across the park's 2,220,000 acres are an estimated 10,000 thermal features. One hundred seven hot spring groups are known. Additional areas probably await discovery. Yellowstone is a hot region. Five percent of the earth's heat radiating from western North America may originate beneath Yellowstone. Only three percent of the park's thermal features are geysers. To qualify as a geyser, a hot spring must intermittently eject water and steam. Conditions producing geysers are fairly rigid.

First, a large heat source is needed. Below the park's geyser fields lies a hot granitic body. Partially molten rock, probably twelve to twenty-four miles deep, heats the granite. Seismic research by geologist Dr. Robert Smith of the University of Utah indicates one portion of the magma chamber may be much closer to the surface. Beneath the Hot Springs Basin Group twelve miles east of Canyon, a partial melt may be within a mile or two of the surface. In regions of North America not exhibiting hot spring activity, magma is normally thirty-five to forty miles below the Earth's surface.

Second, plentiful water is required to prime the geyser's plumbing system. Rain and snow seepage beneath Yellowstone's high plateaus is the source for almost all geyser water, as practically none of the water comes from the magma body. Through faults, tiny fissures, and porous rock, water slowly penetrates as deeply as two miles. At such depths, liquid water may be existing at 663°F, and under pressure of 2,427 pounds per square inch. A minimum of sixty years is usually necessary for the water to reach these depths. Much of Yellowstone's thermal water may have been underground for centuries. The effects of drought or heavy precipitation consequently are averaged over time.

Most geysers do not exhibit seasonal variation.

Third, geysers require natural plumbing that traps hot water before it rises to the surface and cools. Eventually the water becomes so hot that pressure is insufficient to keep it liquid. A steam explosion occurs lifting the water and relieving pressure on the system. Cooler water can then vaporize, triggering a chain reaction of steam explosions. Fountain style geysers like Grand, Great Fountain, and Echinus erupt when large steam bubbles lift water from a surface pool. Cone style geysers like Old Faithful, Castle, and Beehive erupt with a fizzing water and steam mixture, producing a steady water column.

Fourth, geysers occur in rock types that can withstand tremendous temperature and pressure. In Yellowstone the water circulates through volcanic rhyolites and welded ash and tuff. Superheated water dissolves silicon dioxide from the volcanic rock. As pressure drops and water cools, silica, in a form chemically similar to opal, deposits on the geyser's plumbing tube. This action creates the mineral geyserite.

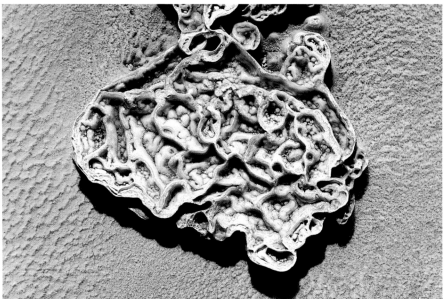

Geyserite deposition eventually seals a geyser. Frequent earthquakes create new routes for superheated water to reach the surface. Assuming that the heat and water supply remains constant, in 1,000 years geysers still will spout across Yellowstone. Features famous today, however, probably will disappear, with new geysers taking their place.

In addition to geysers, Yellowstone has numerous other thermal attractions. At Mammoth Hot Springs, beautiful terraces resemble caves turned inside out.

Silicon dioxide, originating from volcanic rock, is the major source of mineralization in the geyser basins. Called geyserite or siliceous sinter, the deposits may appear like a convoluted brain (below) in the runoff channel from a major geyser. Mammoth Hot Springs lacks true geysers. Thick limestone beds beneath the terraces are the source of calcium carbonate. Filamentous bacteria adhere to islands of freshly deposited travertine (right).

Whether it is Old Faithful (left) or Grand Prismatic Spring (below), Yellowstone contains many of the world's grandest thermal features. A handful of park geysers erupt higher, but nothing diminishes the spectacle of Old Faithful generating a cloud of steam on a frigid October morning. Grand Prismatic is the park's largest spring with a diameter of 370 feet. Its depth has never been plumbed.

Hot water seeping through a thick layer of limestone creates these terraces. The water is saturated with carbon dioxide gas rising from the magma chamber. A hot carbonic acid solution forms that readily dissolves limestone. When the water reaches the surface, it cools and some of the carbon dioxide is lost to the atmosphere. Dissolved limestone then forms a precipitate, the mineral travertine. Terrace growth at Mammoth often occurs quickly with at least two tons of travertine being added daily. Rapidly changing activity occasionally buries forests.

Thousands of hot pools colored from tomato soup red to emerald green dot the park landscape. Vivid colors often result from mineralization. Iron oxides impart reds and browns. Iron pyrites produce grays and blacks. Arsenic sulfides create brilliant yellows and oranges. Elemental sulfur is yellow. As its depth increases, water reflects more blue light, causing color variations in pools.

Thermophilic life is also largely responsible for pool coloration. At temperatures in which humans would perish in seconds, bacteria and blue-green algae thrive. The highest temperature for algae survival in alkaline water is 167°F. Comfortable bath water is 102°F. Hottest temperatures have lemon yellow-colored algae. As water cools, colors blend through orange, red, brown, and green. The belief that boiling kills bacteria is invalid in Yellowstone's superheated water. Pools 5°F above Yellowstone's boiling point of 199°F support multiplying bacteria.

Life in Yellowstone's hot springs is similar to the most primitive forms of algae and bacteria fossilized three billion years ago. Could the park's hot springs be remnants of an environment from the Earth's distant past? Perhaps these tiny organisms are living fossils of life's beginnings. Some scientists theorize that life may have originated in thermal waters, then adapted to other environments.

One of the park's most interesting heat loving bacteria was discovered through the research of Thomas Brock during the 1970s. The organism's name, *Sulfolobus acidocaldarius,* translates from Latin as "a sulfur-using lobe-shaped organism that lives in hot acid environments." *Sulfolobus* obtains energy not from the sun but by oxidizing sulfur to sulfate and sulfuric acid.

Evening Primrose Spring at the western end of Gibbon Meadow is one home for this seemingly unearthly organism. Evening Primrose's temperature can rise to about 195°F, too hot for a healthy *Sulfolobus* population, although a few of the bacteria survive. When heated, the spring's surface is covered with a thick sulfur mat. Gasses welling from below crack the mat and exude fresh yellow sulfur froth. Watching the continually churning sulfurous cauldron is spellbinding. One's imagination needs little encouragement envisioning Evening Primrose's resemblance to a swirling lava lake.

When Evening Primrose cools to 167°F, an optimum temperature for *Sulfolobus* growth, sulfur hungry bacteria completely consume the froth. Evening Primrose also becomes Yellowstone's most acidic spring. With a pH of 0.9, its strong sulfuric acid water could disintegrate clothing.

Acid produced by bacteria and the oxidation of hydrogen sulfide gas that smells like rotten eggs helps create humorous mud pots. Nearly everyone laughs while watching assorted pint-sized features with human expressions plop, explode, and sputter in endless succession. This is caused by acid water decomposing feldspars in volcanic rock to the mineral kaoline or clay. A mud pot is a soupy vat of hot acidic clay. Steam and other gases are trapped by the viscous mud until a "blooping" explosion occurs.

Mud pots are highly dependent on surface water, and their consistency during wet periods is like watery soup. Dry spells make them resemble thick, overcooked porridge. Further drying results in a hissing steam vent or fumarole. Before becoming a fumarole, sailing mud bombs often coat nearby trees,

The floor of a huge mud pot (above) at Mud Volcano domes and explodes producing booms audible for a mile. The expelled contents plaster surrounding vegetation. Such spectacular features are often short-lived. A placid hot spring along the Firehole River (right) probably will last for decades. Vivid colors are from bacteria (white, pink and cream) and algae (orange, brown and green).

boardwalks, and careless spectators. In addition to being quite acidic, the clay acts as a heat compress, and if you are hit, you may receive a nasty burn.

Mudpots occasionally grow to huge proportions. The 1870 Washburn expedition was drawn a half mile by dull, thundering sounds resembling the reports of artillery. The source was a "mud volcano," thirty feet wide and forty feet deep with mud walls thirty-five feet high. Dense masses of steam rising with explosive force from the mudpot's contents hampered the view into the crater. Mud sailing from the "volcano" covered the ground 186 feet away, and tops of lodgepole pines 150 feet above the crater were similarly caked.

More than a century later in 1974 and again in 1980 a similar "mud volcano" was active three quarters of a mile west of the original feature. On still mornings its gutteral explosions were heard a mile into Hayden Valley. Individuals approached this giant's sixty-foot diameter crater with considerable bravery and a degree of foolhardiness. For a distance of 200 feet, mud plastered every tree and blade of grass. In arcing trajectories, irregular globs of mud soared seventy-five feet above the crater rim, then hit with splattering reports.

Twenty-five foot walls constructed of mud bombs sloped steeply into a cauldron. Every few seconds the floor domed and exploded. Steaming, barrel-sized monsters rose ten to twenty feet through the air before collapsing to the crater floor. Late fall of 1980 ended the super mud pot's brief existence, when a lowering water table dried its turbulent contents. In its place roared a foul-smelling steam vent.

Geologic processes are usually thought to occur so slowly that a human lifetime is too brief to witness substantial change. Yet Yellowstone has daily examples of changing geology. The event heralding the great mud pot's 1980 activity was a localized swarm of earthquakes twenty-two to twenty-nine months earlier.

Yellowstone is one of the best places in North America to experience earthquakes. The annual number of felt tremors has ranged between two and 167 in recent years. Many thousands of unfelt events are recorded annually by seismographs monitoring the park.

Most of Yellowstone's tremors are little dish rattlers compared to the strongest earthquake that struck the park during recorded history. This earthquake occurred on the moonlit evening of

August 17, 1959. Epicentered just west of the park, it measured a powerful 7.5 on the Richter scale. Its effects were felt across 500,000 square miles, in eight states and three Canadian provinces.

Although human lives were not lost within the park, twenty-eight people died beneath rock slides west of Yellowstone in the Madison Canyon. The largest slide sent an estimated 43.4 million cubic yards of rock careening across the Madison River. Quake Lake was formed by the landslide, and it remains today, seventeen miles west of the park.

Within Yellowstone, rock fall blocked the Grand Loop road at Firehole Canyon, Gibbon Falls, Virginia Cascades, and Golden Gate. The park's wood buildings creaked and strained, but none collapsed. Chimneys on the Old Faithful Inn and on a few buildings in Mammoth buckled and fell. Guests rapidly vacated

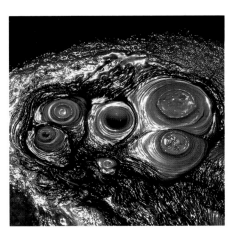

Yellowstone's volcanic rumblings spawn numerous earthquakes. Major tremors dramatically change the landscape. A new spring may develop in a thick lodgepole forest (right). The toppled logs become crisscrossed ghosts in eerie blue water. An acidic lake fed by thermal water may change level (left). Other agents also produce change. Mud pots (above) depend on surface runoff to maintain a soupy consistency. During dry spells they thicken like overcooked porridge.

the old wooden hotels. Partially dressed visitors streamed from the Old Faithful Inn during late evening. Many took unexpected cold showers as a newly installed fire sprinkler system broke, unable to withstand the shaking.

The earthquake was a geologist's dream. Following the main shock, at least 298 geysers erupted. One hundred sixty of these features had not been known to erupt. Four days following the quake, Sapphire Pool at Biscuit Basin began violent 100-foot eruptions, tearing away fifty to 100-pound geyserite "bis-

The most outstanding geologic feature of Yellowstone is the 28 by 47—mile volcanic crater or caldera found in the central portion of the park. Approximately 600,000 years ago an explosion 1,000 times larger than that of Mount St. Helens tore apart Yellowstone. Subsequent lava flows covered most evidence of the blast. North of Canyon, lodgepole pines and lush green meadows now carpet the volcanic rocks. Steep southward facing slopes of the Washburn Range are the caldera's north rim.

cuits" and leaving them stranded fifty feet from the crater. In the Lower Geyser Basin, Clepsydra Geyser began a powerful eruption which since only abates when nearby Fountain Geyser erupts.

Ten thousand thermal features and persistent earthquakes are symptoms of a much larger geologic phenomenon. Across Yellowstone eighty-six percent of the surface rock is volcanic. The region has sustained numerous volcanic outbursts that make recent activity at Mount St. Helens appear minor.

At the end of the mountain building period called the Laramide orogeny, which lifted the Middle Rocky Mountains, came a period of heavy volcanism. About 50 million years ago frequent eruptions deposited beds of volcanic breccias and tuffs 2,000 feet thick in Northern Yellowstone. Mount Washburn's 10,243 foot summit is the eroding remnant of one such volcano.

Twelve miles northeast of Mount Washburn lie portions of Yellowstone's twenty-four and one-half square miles of petrified forests. Along Specimen Ridge many forests lie buried on top of one another in beds of volcanic materials. Standing petrified stumps eroding from the hillside indicate once lush green forests. Many stumps have diameters greater than six feet with well over 500 yearly growth rings. In fine ash, fossilized leaf impressions of sycamores, magnolias, maples, oaks, willows, walnuts, and redwoods tell of a period considerably warmer and wetter than today's mountainous climate. Scientists have identified almost 200 curiously different flowering plants, ten conifers, ten ferns, and three horsetails from the exquisitely preserved fossils.

Mount St. Helens' May 18, 1980 destruction of 200 square miles of Pacific Northwest forests parallels geologic events occurring in Yellowstone approximately 50 million years ago. Similar to Mount St. Helens, volcanoes petrifying Yellowstone's forests had dormant periods lasting many centuries. During quiescent times, lush hardwood forests quickly grew on fertile volcanic soils. Eventually each calm period ended when frequent earthquakes foretold yet another colossal explosion.

With searing heat and hurricane force winds, incandescent ash roared through the forest. Bark was stripped off trunks, and trees snapped like toothpicks. Mud flows carried stumps and logs miles from their origin. Many feet of volcanic debris accumulated from ominous black lightning strewn clouds. A stark gray landscape was created where once life had been bountiful. While new forests renewed their grip across devastated lands, water circulated through underlying debris. Silica dissolved from the ash and filled cavities within and between wood cells. The wood was petrified so perfectly that minor cell structure may be observed 50 million years later.

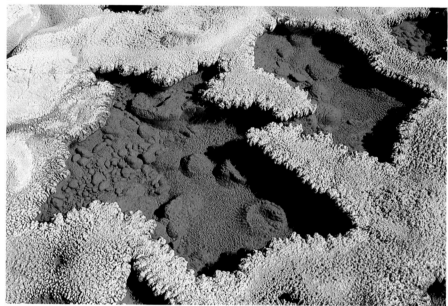

Following the Absaroka volcanics came a long period of volcanic quiet that ended 2.2 million years ago. For approximately 200,000 years, the Yellowstone Plateau bulged as a magma chamber melted into the crust. Fractures penetrating the crust allowed molten rock to swell to the surface, and small flows of rhyolite spread from the bulge. Rhyolite is a rapidly cooled volcanic rock with mineral composition similar to granite but having a finer crystal structure. At some critical time, lava flows sufficiently reduced pressure on the magma chamber to cause a cataclysmic eruption. In a matter of minutes, well over 600 cubic miles of fragmented material, ash, and hot gasses crossed thousands of square miles obliterating all life in its path. Suddenly releasing much of its contents, the magma chamber collapsed. This created a huge crater known as a caldera.

The explosion dwarfs the blast of Mount St. Helens by a scale of 2,500 times. Even the 1883 catastrophic explosion of the East Indies island of Krakatoa was 140 times smaller than this first Yellowstone blast. Krakatoa's eruption sent dust clouds sailing fifty miles high and was distinctly heard in Australia 3,000 miles away. Twelve square miles were destroyed, leaving the island

Rain and snow supplies almost all the water in Yellowstone's geysers. The water slowly circulates as deep as two miles where it is subjected to great temperature and pressure. Under such extreme conditions silicon dioxide becomes soluble. When the water resurfaces, the silicon dioxide is deposited in a form similar to opal, creating jeweled beauty around the geysers (above and right). Eventually the deposition seals a spring shut. Earthquakes open new cracks from which springs emerge.

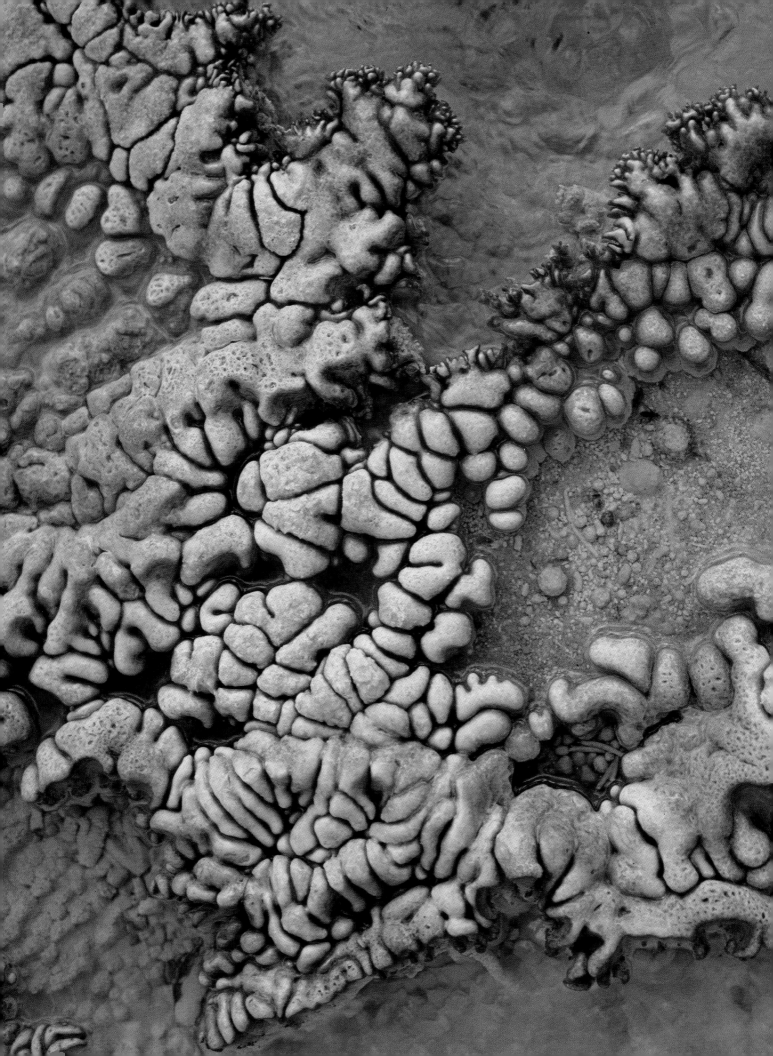

one-third its former size.

Yellowstone's eruption 2 million years ago set the stage for two subsequent explosions that largely erased evidence of the initial event. One million two hundred thousand years ago ejection of approximately ninety-six cubic miles of material forged the second caldera. North of Ashton, Idaho, a long hill is the volcano's southern flank, and at the crest there is a drop into a large circular crater encompassing Island Park. Subsequent basaltic lava flows cover much of the crater floor.

Six hundred thousand years ago came Yellowstone's most recent calamitous explosion. Remnants of its twenty-eight by forty-seven mile crater lie within central portions of the park. Similar to the

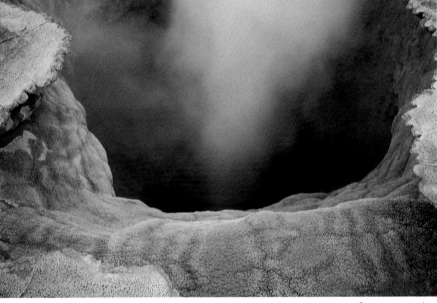

Forces of nature collide as boiling water from erupting Castle Geyser encounters icy air on a morning that is 45°F below zero (left). The geyser basins become surrealistic scenes of contrasting elements during winter cold spells. In all seasons, Yellowstone's major geysers assert their strength. Following a 150-foot eruption, the crater of Giantess Geyser (above) jets steam from its black depths with an ear-splitting roar.

earlier calderas, pressure from a growing subsurface magma body domed and cracked the surface. A double set of ring-like fractures allowed rhyolitic lava intermittently to escape for 600,000 years before the blast. When lava melted through the entire ring fracture system, conditions were prime for another devastating explosion.

The blast came in two parts. A surge of ash, pumice, and rock debris swept across the Yellowstone Plateau, riding on hot expanding gasses. When the ash flows settled, particles fused, forming a hard welded tuff with a rhyolitic composition. Probably within hours of the first huge eruption came a second explosion, indicating two closely situated magma bodies were present. Nearly 240 cubic miles of debris were ejected approximating 1,000 Mount St. Helens. Atmospherically carried fragments of the blast have been recovered more than 1,000 miles away in Saskatchewan, Texas, and

California. Over 30 feet of ash accumulated in parts of the Oklahoma panhandle.

The event annihilated the southern extent of the Washburn Range. The caldera rim is easily visible north of Canyon where Hedges and Dunraven Peaks end abruptly in steep south-facing slopes. Thirty miles south, Flat Mountain and the Red Mountains mark the caldera's opposite boundary.

The great blister forged in the Yellowstone Plateau oozed lava for hundreds of thousands of years. Consequently, much of the caldera has been filled by rhyolitic flows. North of the confluence of the Firehole and Gibbon Rivers, towering slopes of Purple Mountain are the caldera's northwest boundary. Across the Madison River, National Park Mountain and the edge of the Madison Plateau abruptly rise 800 feet. The escarpment is formed because the 105,000-year-old West Yellowstone flow did not reach the caldera border. Here the Madison River flows through a canyon initiated by tremendous volcanic activity. As recently as 70,000 years ago magma has erupted on the surface. This raises the question: Is volcanic activity again likely on the Yellowstone Plateau?

Visitors frequently ask if Old Faithful is slowing down, or if the park's interior is cooling. People may sense powerful geyser displays are only the tip of Yellowstone's potential. They seek reassurance that the park is quieting and will not blow its top. Yellowstone, however, could be preparing for another inferno. Intervals between previous explosions have been 800,000 and 600,000 years. It is not consoling to know the last blast was 600,000 years ago.

In recent years, the three and a half mile trek from Old Faithful to Mallard Lake has become a bit steeper. Ground to the east of Mallard Lake is sporadically rising, some years bulging upward at a rate of a half inch a year. A similar bulge or resurgent dome is situated at Lee Hardy Rapids north of Yellowstone Lake. One possible cause could be pressure from a subterranean magma body. However, if Yellowstone repeats geologic history, we should have advance warning. Prolonged increases in geyser activity may signal a rising heat source, and intense earthquake swarms, including harmonic tremors, would indicate movement of liquid rock beneath the surface. Slow moving rhyolite flows should precede any major blast.

The magnitude of Yellowstone's volcanic activity is comparable to Iceland or Hawaii. One thousand miles east of the Pacific rim of fire, it may seem odd to find so much activity. Mount St. Helens, Mount Shasta, Mount Rainier, and Mount Hood and the San Andreas Fault are evidence of two great plates of the earth grinding past each other. Giant convection currents within the mantle pull North America past the plate on which the Pacific Ocean rests. Because they are on opposite sides of the plate boundary, Los Angeles and San Francisco will eventually pass one another.

Yellowstone may be the focus of a long tear trending northeast from the plate boundary. As North America slips past the Pacific plate, differing speeds of movement may be fracturing the continent into a series of subplates. Visualize the Pacific plate as a block of gelatin and the North American plate as a tray of ice cubes with the tray and divider removed. Take the ice and attempt to slide it along the side of the gelatin. At first, the ice cubes will stick to the gelatin. Then, as pressure increases, the ice will suddenly slide, simulating a major earthquake. As the ice cubes move along at different speeds, gaps develop between them. In this manner, North America may be fracturing into subplates.

During the past 18 million years, a tear has moved up the Snake River Plain with its terminus now in Yellowstone. To the northeast, a lateral tear has moved into Oregon ending near the Newberry Caldera. Yellowstone's heat source seems to be moving northeasterly at one and one-half inches per year. Perhaps a giant opening zipper relieving continental growth pains will eventually create a Yellowstone-type park in Canada. Following numerous caldera-creating explosions, the current rate of movement will place Yellowstone's heat source across the Saskatchewan border in 21 million years.

66 This reserve is a natural breeding-
ground and nursery for those stately and
beautiful haunters of the wilds which
have now vanished from so many of the
great forests, the vast lonely plains, and
the high mountain ranges, where they
once abounded. **99**

Theodore Roosevelt
1903

White patches of yampa blossoms sprinkle Yellowstone's large open meadows by mid-July. In the higher reaches of Hayden Valley among the white flowers, a significant portion of Yellowstone's buffalo live. Here, far from the roadside crowds, ancient rutting rituals begin. For approximately a month while the cows come into heat, bulls become exceedingly agitated. From mixed groups of animals, bulls create a cacophony of menacing bellows and grunts. Yelowstone hikers occasionally mistake a rutting bison's growl for an angered grizzly bear.

An individual observing bison in midsummer should give battling bulls the same margin of distance as a grizzly. Most disputes are settled through evil stares, head bobbing threats, and short charges, when the subordinate male turns tail and runs. But when two bulls of similar status cannot settle their differences through energy conserving nasty looks, a vicious fight ensues.

Grinding hooves fling clods of soil as two animals charge. In a cloud of dust, two tons of flesh and bones collide. Two heads crashing send a resounding thud across the meadow. The tussle may end following quick horn jabs, or the bulls may engage in a shoving match where horns lock for twenty seconds or more. Almost never does an encounter end in death, although many old bulls exhibit numerous battle scars. Vicious as the battles appear, they are essential in assuring that the strongest bulls mate and contribute their genetic background to succeeding generations.

The Park Service discourages travel across Hayden Valley in order to furnish bison and grizzly bears undisturbed countryside. One August day I learned the effect a single human could have upon hundreds of bison, and conversely what effect hundreds of bison could have on a single human. My trail followed the abandoned Trout Creek Road, once a thoroughfare for stagecoaches traveling between the former Fountain Flats Hotel and Canyon and later used as a fire road. In remote sections of Hayden Valley, quantities of black, grass-filled grizzly bear dung left me somewhat nervous.

The wildlife too was skittish. In contrast to roadside animals which become tolerant of humans, backcountry wildlife often run from people. A herd of more than 100 elk ended their morning grazing, becoming a wave of racing flesh as I was detected a quarter of a mile away.

As I climbed toward Mary Mountain, open stands of lodgepole pine encroached on spacious meadows. Signs of bison became omnipresent. Every tree was partially girdled from decades of bison rubbing their bodies and polishing their horns. Buffalo chips littered the ground between circular wallows that smelled strongly of urine. An occasional lodgepole sapling lay on its side, uprooted by the horns of an ornery bull.

I came upon small bands of cows and calves tended by bellowing bulls. Climbing over the top of a grassy knoll, the next depression was carpeted with perhaps 250 grazing bison. Following the trail into the depression, I passed 500 feet south of the herd before the animals sensed my presence. The closest individuals exhibited signs of typical bison nervousness—raised tails followed by defecation. A few cows bolted away, triggering the herd into thundering motion.

At the same time the bison stampeded over a ridge to the north, branches snapped and cracked in the lodgepole forest to the south. Within seconds,

another group of fifty animals charged from the forest trying to catch up with the departing herd. Finding myself in the path of the onrushing animals, I looked for a lodgepole pine to climb. The closest tree was 200 feet away, too far to reach before grinding hooves were upon me.

Suppressing my vision of being caught beneath stampeding bison, I remembered that the Plains Indians would stake out a wildly jumping and scream-

Frost covers sagebrush and lone bison (right) on a crisp October morning in Hayden Valley. The frost signals many months of harsh winter. Ribs showing in late fall may indicate that this old bull will feed coyotes before spring. As the winter snow melts, a group of cow bison (below) feed on the previous summer's vegetation. When meadows become green in May, the cows will drop their ruddy calves.

ing person to split a flowing herd. I faced the charging bison and in a frenzy, jumped, waved, and screamed. The bison rushing directly at me stopped their charge in confusion. To avoid a pileup, those stampeding from behind swerved to miss their confused companions. The stalled animals then saw their compeers galloping on both sides of me and followed suit.

As the rumbling of galloping hooves waned, I became aware that the pounding of my heart was nearly as noisy. Twice I have scurried up trees to avoid inquisitive grizzly bears, but never have I been as frightened as when fifty bison bore down upon me.

Naturalist Ernest Seton-Thompson estimated that 60 million bison lived on the North American continent in 1800. Their original range stretched from Alaska to Georgia. By 1900 mass extermination of these magnificent animals reduced the wild population to probably less than 300 of which 250 lived north of the border in Canada.

Most of us learn in school that buffalo were killed to fulfill human needs for food, skins, clothing, or sport. A more truthful reason for the slaughter of millions of these great animals was to deprive the Plains Indians of their primary food source and force them to the reservations. Most carcasses were left to rot in the hot prairie sun.

But Yellowstone was so remote that a remnant population of the wild mountain bison race survived. The enabling act which created Yellowstone as a park in 1872 did not provide protection for the park's abundant wildlife, since the legislation only spoke against the "wanton destruction" of game. Gentlemen sport hunting was allowed as was the procurement of wild meat for camp. Bison, which had been systematically destroyed over the rest of North America, provided a lucrative target as their heads brought $100 to $300 each.

On March 12, 1894, notorious Cooke City poacher Ed Howell was captured in Pelican Valley after he had slaughtered at least eleven buffalo for their heads and robes. Public outcry, spearheaded by the conservation voice of *Forest and*

Stream, persuaded Congress to pass the Lacey Act twenty-six days following Howell's arrest. The legislation mandated strict sentences for poaching and saved Yellowstone's bison.

Following the Lacey Act, a limited amount of poaching continued. Wild bison numbers fell to a count of twenty-three in 1902 although a larger population of forty to fifty animals probably was scattered throughout the park. From numbers which ranked in the millions, this was the last vestige of completely wild bison left in the United States.

To help augment the wild population, the park administration decided in 1902 to introduce a captive herd of twenty-one plains bison at Mammoth Hot Springs. Five years later the group was moved to the Lamar Valley where they prospered under ranching practices. By the 1920s the semidomestic animals were allowed to mingle with the park's original wild bison. The present day population is a hybrid of mountain and plains races.

The saga of bison in Yellowstone is one of success. The species was brought from near extinction to a current population of more than 2,500 within park borders. Trumpeter swans have a similar history. By 1930 the ravages of the plume

trade and market hunting had reduced these magnificent white birds. Thirty nesting pairs occupying the land in and around Yellowstone were the remaining trumpeter population in the lower forty-eight states. Protection by Yellowstone, along with Grand Teton National Park and Red Rock Lakes National Wildlife Refuge, saved trumpeter swans from disappearing south of Canada.

Not only does Yellowstone National Park protect species threatened elsewhere, it also is an example of natural environments operating without human influence. Yellowstone is a living laboratory where a policy of "no management" is the preferred management. When given the opportunity, people

Elk and bison congregate in thermal areas (left) when winter descends on the park. The snow may be four to five feet deep in the lodgepole forests. But along the Firehole River, warmer ground allows easier access to forage. Winter food availability limits the numbers of many park species. During the bounty of summer, a coyote pup (above, right) surveys the world from the entrance of its den.

leave their mark upon the land through manipulation. Across America wildlife is "managed" through harvesting, feeding, and habitat improvements. Our species selects for those animals we view as "good" and attempts to eliminate those species considered "bad." Early days in Yellowstone saw managers placing similar labels on wildlife. Bison and elk were supplementally fed, while wolves and mountain lions were unmercifully pursued, trapped and shot. At least 121 mountain lions and 136 wolves were killed during the period from 1904 to 1926. A small population of mountain lions still survives; however, the Rocky Mountain wolf was totally lost from the ecosystem. To restore Yellowstone's balance of predators and prey, park managers and wildlife biologists hope to reintroduce wolves into Yellowstone soon.

Today in Yellowstone, value labels are no longer placed upon wildlife. Instead, all native fauna is considered part of the working ecosystem. Park managers realize that Yellowstone's wildlife survived for thousands of years without human intervention. Continued survival seems assured by making corrections for past mistakes and allowing natural factors to prevail.

Visitors to Yellowstone seeing large elk congregations occasionally ask what the park does to regulate their number. Following a series of mild winters, the summer Yellowstone elk herd may swell to 31,000. In the late fall, the elk separate into several wintering groups both inside and outside park borders. Elk leaving the park are subject to population control through regulated hunting and artificial feeding. They also face habitat loss as traditional winter range is fenced off for cattle grazing, home sites and other human development. Severe winters will cause large numbers of elk to migrate north of the park toward Paradise Valley. Many of the southern elk travel to the Jackson Hole Elk Refuge. Smaller groups winter in several scattered locations. A resident herd remains within the vicinity of the Firehole, Gibbon, and Upper Madison Rivers. In all 13,000 to 15,000 elk generally winter within Yellowstone.

Elk feed in snow country by pawing away winter's mantle to reach dried grasses and sedges. To avoid digging through snow, they seek windswept ridges and thermal areas. Among hot springs, green grass can be found growing even during January's icy spells. When the snow becomes excessively

deep and especially when an icy crust caps the snow, malnutrition combined with other stresses kills many elk. Following the fires and severe drought of 1988, an estimated 3,500 to 6,400 elk perished. At first thought it may seem cruel —thousands of elk left to starve a lingering death in Yellowstone's icy cold. Yet that always has been nature's way.

Before the coming of European man to

Yellowstone, no one provided elk emergency rations. Native Americans did not practice mercy killing. Winter quietly and efficiently culled the weak, old, sick, and injured, leaving the strongest animals to reproduce. When elk and bison die in winter, their carcasses are often completely consumed in less than 48 hours.

For the coyotes, ravens, pine martens, bald eagles, gray jays, and other scavengers, winter kill provides meat needed to survive Yellowstone's long, harsh winters. In March and April, when the grizzly bears end their winter slumber, ninety percent of their diet is carrion or weakened elk which are easily killed. When considered in these terms, an elk perishes to provide sustenance to a grizzly bear. Instead of death, the process may be thought of as nature's cycle of life passing on to life.

Carcasses not discovered by winter scavengers are utilized during the warm days of spring and summer. Thousands of invertebrates chew their way through the decomposing flesh. Multitudes of insects attract hungry chipping sparrows, yellow-rumped warblers, garter snakes and others. The cycle of

The Firehole River provides easy travel when deep snow covers meadows and forests. A cow and calf elk (left) feed on aquatic vegetation nurtured by warm water. Shallow sections of the Yellowstone River in Hayden Valley are prime summer moose habitat (right). Bulls grow impressive antlers during summer's warm days. The velvet covering conceals arteries that bring nourishment to the growing rack.

Canada geese are year round park residents. Thermal water that keeps rivers open and warm ground that allows grass to grow even in January entice geese to endure Yellowstone's winters. Along the Firehole River geese frequently graze with bison and elk. Here a flock takes flight after feeding at warm ground near Artemisia Geyser.

life passing to life is complete when nutrients washed into the soil leave the grass slightly greener for many years.

If the park were to assist the elk through supplemental feeding or by killing excess animals as was done in the past, who would provide the food for all the predators and scavengers? Instead, park managers allow natural processes to occur.

One factor which greatly assists Yellowstone's elk and buffalo is approximately 10,000 thermal features and associated warm ground. Consider sleeping upon snow when the night temperature plunges to 40°F below zero. Precious comfort and energy conservation can be obtained by seeking a warm patch where the surface temperature might be 100°F above zero. Elk reclining on such hot spots rise in the morning with two-toned coats. Their side that was against warm ground is chocolate brown, while their other side exposed to icy air is coated with a frost crystal fleece.

When the snow is four to six feet deep, locking the summer's grass beneath a white robe, Yellowstone's grazers drain their energy while attempting to walk and feed. In the geyser basins, warm

A bull elk attentively listens to a rival's bugles across Elk Park (left). Through September and October bulls spar with one another, establishing dominance for mating with harems of cows. Bighorn rams (below) perform their rutting in December. The sharp reports of butting horns echo off the rolling hills near Gardiner. Rutting battles ensure that the strongest males pass their genetic background to succeeding generations.

ground melts vast quantities of snow, allowing easy access to forage. Hot spring-fed rivers generally do not freeze and provide snow-free avenues of travel. During most winter days, elk warm their legs in the Firehole, Gibbon, and Madison rivers while they act like summertime moose feeding upon aquatic vegetation. But geyser basins are limited in available food resources. If severe weather cuts off peripheral grazing areas, Yellowstone coyotes feast.

Hundreds of elk and bison spend each winter near boiling hot springs and geysers. It is surprising that more do not break thin crust or fall into scalding pools. Most years one or two elk and bison end their lives in boiling water. Consequently many pool bottoms are littered with bones. The animals, however, generally know where it is safe to walk among the hot springs. Many more elk and bison survive Yellowstone's harsh winters because of the output of thermal energy than the few animals that perish in the pools.

When an animal is cooked in a hot spring, its body gives nourishment to bacteria which thrive in the boiling water. Occasionally large carnivores attempt to fish out and eat the cooked flesh.

One summer a park ranger observed a startled group of bison stampeding past superheated Ojo Caliente Spring. Movement of the herd caused one of the peripheral bulls to be pushed into the boiling water. The bull attempted to climb from the pool but was unable to scale an overhanging ledge, and within a minute, the bull succumbed to the boiling water. The next day the ranger returned to see what had happened to the carcass. He was surprised to find that the aroma from the boiled meat had lured a large grizzly bear to Ojo Caliente's edge. From time to time, the bruin would reach out and attempt to tear off a hunk of hot meat from the bloated carcass. In the process the bear would scald its paw and run back into nearby trees to cool it off before returning to the spring for another attempt to feed.

A grizzly trying to devour a naturally boiled bison is the way of nature. A roadside black bear panhandling tidbits from passing motorists is not. Just as the park management does not assist the elk and bison through severe winters, the policy of keeping a natural working ecosystem does not allow humans to feed bears.

Bears, like Old Faithful, are a symbol of Yellowstone National Park. In the past, visitors touring the Grand Loop Road would drive from bear-caused traffic jam to traffic jam. Counts of thirty to sixty black bears seen during a family's Yellowstone outing were common. At any time a substantial portion of the park's black bears were working the roadsides, while numerous grizzly bears regularly frequented dumps.

Clearly an unnatural situation was occurring. Numerous black bears were accidentally hit by passing motorists. In the dumps, huge concentrations of grizzlies allowed the boars, or male grizzlies, to occasionally kill and cannibalize cubs. Park records reveal that an annual average of forty-five people were bitten or mauled by park bears.

The year 1970 was the turning point in bear management. Attempting to return to natural conditions, park administrators decided that all human food sources must be removed from bears. Park dumps were permanently closed and visitors were fined for feeding bears or leaving an unclean campsite. Bears that went to developed areas searching for handouts were captured and transported to the backcountry. Incorrigibles that repeatedly returned following relocations were sent to zoos or were killed.

Within ten years Yellowstone had a population of grizzly and black bears which generally did not know humans were easy targets for food. When visitors come to Yellowstone today, observing a wild bear is an uncommon treat. The Interagency Grizzly Bear Study Team estimates more than 200 grizzlies inhabit the greater Yellowstone area, which includes the park and surrounding suitable habitat on State and Federal lands. A healthy population of black bears exists within the same region. Interestingly, recent population estimates are similar to figures cited during the bear feeding era. At that time most Yellowstone bears were frequenting the one percent of developed park lands. With bears now utilizing natural foods, most roam wildlands far from roads. The day of the roadside begging bear has been replaced with the opportunity of glimpsing a wild bear in its natural habitat.

One morning outside my window, two grizzlies charged across Porcelain Basin in pursuit of a cow and calf elk. Just 100 feet from my house the grizzlies pulled down the bleating calf, killed it, and in twenty minutes stripped the carcas clean of meat. A half mile away the Norris Campground presented easy pickings, yet these two bears spent all spring and early summer preying upon young elk. In the far reaches of the Norris Geyser Basin, we found evidence of another kill site from this pair of grizzlies. Tracks in the soft mud told the story of a calf elk chased into a small scalding pool. Pieces of fur-covered flesh floating in the spring lent evidence that the calf had partially cooked before the grizzlies succeeded in pulling it from the pool. They dragged the carcass thirty feet, then consumed all but three vertebrae.

Yellowstone lore is ingrained with similar wildlife tales. Each person who visits the park takes home special memories of animals who do not fear humans but instead share a great park. Thousands of miles of driving to the park can be made worthwhile by an hour watching a velvet-covered bull moose feed in the Yellowstone River. And perhaps the trip to Yellowstone is worth even more when a gray jay alights on one's shoulder to survey the family picnic.

66 Its upper waters flow through
deep cañons and gorges, and are broken by
immense cataracts and fearful rapids,
presenting at various points some of the
grandest scenery on the continent. **99**

Nathaniel P. Langford
1871

The Lower Falls of the Yellowstone River, plummetting 308 feet, lay shrouded in white. A drifting cloud of ice fog veils the upper half of the falls. The ice shield grows slowly from the canyon floor. On an icy, sub-zero February morning, this winter cover rises past the 150-foot mark.

Each winter the white cone seeks parity with the 300-foot cliff over which the Yellowstone River tumbles. Lengthening warmer days of April doom the effort. The ice cone collapses into a barrage of icebergs, bobbing and crashing down river. One might imagine the falls frozen like the surrounding landscape if it were not for the muffled roar of 15,000 gallons of water rushing each second through a gaping hole in the base of the ice cone.

The Yellowstone River, for a few moments, plunges through a realm that no one can see. Clusters of blue glazed cauliflowers grow toward the rushing water. Within the ice cone, water shoots through a wild, crystalline sculptured chamber. Its magnificent icicle draped grottoes, illuminated in eerie blue, can only be imagined. Nature makes this spot inaccessible. Three hundred feet downstream, the river emerges from an icy, cavernous world to begin a tumultuous twenty-mile journey through the Grand Canyon of the Yellowstone.

From my vantage spot at Artist Point, the ice cone looks like a mound of sugar. Murmurs of rapids 1,200 feet below mingle with the dampened roar of the falls a mile upstream. Complementing muted sounds, the air is motionless. Its stillness is appreciated on this chilly morning. The tranquility is broken by a rush of wind around avian wings. Twenty-five feet below, a bald eagle glides past the rock outcrops of Artist Point. Even the canyon's vastness cannot dwarf the eagle's size. The immense bird flies so close, I can see its yellow eyes. I marvel at how near the eagle has approached. Perhaps eagles watch beneath them for man-caused danger and do not consider a person above them threatening. Perhaps this bird recognizes the sanctuary Yellowstone offers.

As the eagle flies up the canyon toward the Lower Falls, I notice its flight has a wave-like fluidity. Each strong downbeat is nearly complete when the previous upbeat's pulse reaches the wing tip. Observed on the same plane, the long wings undulate as energy flows through them.

I feel exhilarated when I look upon the eagle's flight. For a few seconds, my spirit is airborne as I realize my view is comparable to that of the eagle. But, as the great bird maneuvers from sight through the canyon's crooks and declivities, my feet suddenly become heavy.

The encounter with the eagle brings memories of another morning at Artist Point four winters earlier. On that day, I watched a raven fly past my vantage point on the canyon rim. It is common to find ravens in the Grand Canyon of the Yellowstone. Strong updrafts, pinnacles for roosting, and numerous nooks make the canyon an ideal habitat.

The big black bird's manner of flight was unusual. When I first saw it, the raven was a black object with wings folded, racing toward the canyon's bottom. Before plunging into the river, the bird extended its wings pulling up from the Earth in a graceful curve. At the apex of its ascent, the raven spoke a resounding "groark," then tucked its wings in a manner causing it to flip over. Completing the roll, the raven's wings remained folded, and it again dove to-

ward the river. The aerobatics were repeated many times before the bird faded from sight in the mist of Lower Falls.

I doubt the raven was exhibiting flight skill to a prospective mate. The bird flew alone and directly up the canyon. I conclude that the flying demonstration was done for sheer joy. Science tells us not to attribute human feelings to the animal kingdom, yet what other explanation can there be? Is enjoying the incredible

The Yellowstone River changes mood when it ends its gentle meanderings and drops through rapids toward the Upper Falls (left). The frothing water leaps 109 feet before continuing a half mile journey to the Lower Falls. After racing through pillars of volcanic tuff and breccia, water tumbles over 132-foot Tower Fall (right). The boulder at its brink stood fast for more than a century before being swept over the falls in the spring of 1986.

beauty of the Grand Canyon a right reserved only for our species?

Few humans have attemped touring Yellowstone's Grand Canyon from an eagle's or raven's vista. The Park Service strictly forbids flying and hang gliding in the canyon because of obvious safety hazards and the imposition on the Grand Canyon's wildness.

Nevertheless, pilots occasionally lower their aircraft between the walls of the

Fine spray from 197-foot Fairy Falls dresses its cliff with skirts of blue and white ice (left) during the long Yellowstone winter. It is the natural property of ice to reflect blue light. In summer spray from Crystal Falls feeds a collection of ferns (above). Lush vegetation flourishes near Yellowstone's approximately one hundred and fifty waterfalls.

canyon. At the brink of the Upper Falls, two lodgepole pines bear the scars of one such attempt. In August 1974, four Air Force pilots rented a single engine Piper aircraft and illegally descended into the canyon. Instead of flying downstream and taking advantage of the canyon's lowering elevation, they flew up canyon toward the two towering falls. Approaching the Lower Falls, a strong downdraft wrenched the plane toward the frothing cataract. Despite pulling up at full throttle, the aircraft fell at a rate of 800 feet per minute. It cleared the Lower Falls.

The next obstacle came a half mile ahead. Close to the Upper Falls, a second sharp downdraft again pushed the aircraft toward disaster. It barely missed some twenty people in the observation area at the brink of the Upper Falls. The pilot tried to avoid trees lining both sides of the narrow Yellowstone River. He clipped two lodgepole pines along the right bank and crashed in the Yellowstone River approximately 400 yards above the falls. Fortunately the plane lodged on rocks along the left bank. After a few tense minutes, the

door swung open, revealing that everyone inside was safe. Had the accident occurred a few weeks earlier when the river was higher, the wreckage probably would have been swept over the falls.

Viewed from the canyon rim, the Yellowstone River is a green and white ribbon winding between gigantic pink, orange, yellow, and brown walls. Piece by piece, the river has transported enormous quantities of rock, creating a cathedral 750 to 1,600 feet deep, 1,000 to 4,000 feet wide and twenty miles long. Formation of Yellowstone's Grand Canyon involves a complex and repetitive combination of volcanism, glaciation, hydrothermal rock alteration, and erosion. The canyon's birth probably is traceable to an ancestral river drainage cutting south from the present junction of the Lamar and Yellowstone rivers.

The upper seven miles of the Grand Canyon lay within the tremendous explosion crater blasted from the central portion of Yellowstone National Park 600,000 years ago. The volcanic explosion and subsequent caldera collapse destroyed the previous river drainage within the caldera. North of the caldera, many feet of volcanic material buried the ancestral river but probably left a depression for a future river.

Water collected within the caldera, creating a lake many times larger than present Yellowstone Lake. For thousands of years this lake likely drained west through an outlet near present Madison Junction. Approximately 150,000 years ago volcanoes beneath the lake built a rhyolite and tuff ridge, splitting the caldera lake into east and west sections. This volcanic action created Mary Mountain and the Central Plateau. Cut from its western drainage, the eastern caldera lake rose, and rhyolite flows again split it into north and south lakes. The northern lake reached an altitude of 8,000 feet and was probably the first water draining north along the present course of the Yellowstone River. Tucked between Red Rock Point and the Grand Canyon's north rim, remnants of this early stage form a paleocanyon whose ancient bottom is 250 feet above the present river level.

Between 85,000 and 120,000 years ago, the Bull Lake glacial period occurred. From the Absaroka Mountains, great ice masses flowed north and west, merging into an ice cap with a maximum depth over 3,000 feet. Early during the glaciation, ice moving down the Lamar River Valley flowed south into the Yellowstone

55

River drainage. The flow blocked the Yellowstone River, creating a lake which deposited more than 200 feet of sediments within the canyon next to Red Rock Point. Stagnant ice soon filled the canyon. Lack of ice movement saved the canyon from being ground into another glacier scoured U-shaped valley common to the Rocky Mountains. After about 10,000 years, the glaciers retreated, leaving the Grand Canyon vulnerable to down cutting.

The erosion may have been catastrophic. Approximately 100,000 years ago, another lava flow erupted beneath the ice-free northern caldera lake. Displaced water from the vicinity of Hayden Valley probably caused a flood within the Grand Canyon. Before the Bull Lake glacial period ended, a second ice advance again dammed the canyon. One hundred fifty feet of sediment were left west of Inspiration Point where water ponded against ice. Following the final melting of Bull Lake glaciers, erosive agents widened and deepened the canyon for approximately 60,000 years.

Geologic history was repeated when Pinedale Glaciation began approximately 25,000 years ago. An ice cap eventually thickened to 3,000 feet in the Yellowstone Lake Basin, and from the northeast, a river of ice also flowed toward the canyon. Glacial Boulder, a giant erratic of Precambrian gneiss, was carried from the Beartooth Mountains. It now rests near Inspiration Point on the Grand Canyon's north rim. The rock measures twenty-four by twenty by eighteen feet and weighs over 1 million pounds.

As with the previous Bull Lake glaciation, ice entered and filled the Grand Canyon but did not scour it. When the ice finally melted releasing trapped water in Yellowstone Lake, evidence points toward yet another great flood. Millions of tons of rock were moved downstream undercutting the canyon's walls and deepening the gorge.

Geologists believe it has taken the Yellowstone River only 160,000 years to carve its magnificent gorge. Spectacular erosion has been aided by fractures deeply penetrating hot rock. Steam and hot water rise to the surface. Hot spring activity beginning immediately downstream from the Lower Falls greatly weakens the rhyolite. Hydrothermally altered rhyolite is highly erodable. Much harder, unaltered rhyolite forms the escarpment of the Lower Falls. Vivid yellow, pink, and red hues staining the Grand Canyon are also products of hydrothermal alteration.

Rhyolite is normally a drab gray to brown. Iron oxides leeching from decomposing rhyolite give the coloration.

Through careful observation, geyser activity often can be observed along the canyon's bottom from the Lower Falls to beyond Artist Point. High water during spring and summer drowns many of the vents. When the water level drops, at least seven features may play, shooting boiling water into the river. The largest spouter, located below Artist Point, erupts to a respectable forty feet but is dwarfed by the Grand Canyon's enormous size.

A half mile upstream from the Lower Falls are the Upper Falls, whose formation was not caused by hydrothermal activity. Differing hardness in two lava flows created the 109 foot drop. Above the falls the rhyolite is dense and resists erosion. Below the falls the rhyolite is made brittle by a high percentage of volcanic glass. Rapid cooling, probably the result of lava encountering a cold lake, caused the molten rock to become glassy.

The magnificent Upper and Lower Falls are but two of approximately fifty named waterfalls and cascades found within Yellowstone National Park. More than 100 seldom visited waterfalls, remote in Yellowstone's backcountry, remain unnamed.

Averaging 8,000 feet elevation, the Yellowstone region receives enough rain and snow to feed a vast network of

The Yellowstone River plummets 308 feet over the Lower Falls (right). Hot spring activity has greatly weakened the rhyolite downstream from the falls, allowing the river to carve a magnificent chasm through highly erodible rock. Red Rock Point (left) looms above the Yellowstone River. The hanging canyon to the left of the point is an earlier path of the Yellowstone River. On moist autumn mornings, spider webs close to the canyon hang heavy with water droplets (above).

Spray from the Lower Falls drifts skyward on a cool fall day, enhancing the beauty of the Grand Canyon of the Yellowstone. Brown and red pillars of altered rhyolite owe their colors to iron oxides. Lodgepole pines dig their roots into precariously steep slopes. Many trees will slide down the canyon as erosive agents widen and deepen the gorge. Landslides are common within the canyon, especially after the park has been rattled by earthquakes.

streams and rivers. The Continental Divide, that spine of the continent separating the Atlantic and Pacific watersheds, crosses Yellowstone National Park. Precipitation falling over the park flows to both oceans. Water begins its journey to the Atlantic through the Yellowstone, Gallatin, and Madison river systems. It drains to the Pacific via the Snake and Falls rivers.

Except for an arid rain shadow stretching from Lamar Valley to the North Entrance, most of the park receives twenty to forty inches of precipitation annually. Above the Mirror, Madison, and Pitchstone plateaus and along the Gallatin and Absaroka mountains, moisture laden southwest winds rise and cool. In these high elevations, annual precipitation soars to fifty to eighty inches. During winter, 400 to 600 inches of snow falls.

High volcanic plateaus, originating from at least forty separate lava flows, contain many cliffs over which melted snow and rain water tumble. In the southwest portion of the park called Cascade Corner, drainages of the Falls and Bechler rivers account for about fifty waterfalls. Lush vegetation, reminiscent of the Pacific Northwest, and plentiful cascading streams leave a pleasant veneer on ancient, seething rhyolite flows. Since Cascade Corner is so remote, many of the region's thundering waterfalls were not discovered and named until 1920.

Union Falls, one of Cascade Corner's prettiest, drops 250 feet over hundreds of terraced ledges. Two forks of Mountain Ash Creek merge at the falls in a silky frothing mass. Water slamming into boulders sends icy spray hundreds of feet downstream. Even on the hottest summer days, bushwacking to the base of Union Falls is uncomfortably cold. Backpackers may reach the falls along established but strenuous trails. Nestled deep within the backcountry, most of Cascade Corner's falls are in remote wilderness canyons.

Although one can hike cross country and see falls that may not have been viewed for more than a decade, many spectacular falls are easily accessible from park roads. Tower Fall, located along the Grand Loop Road's northeast corner, is one of Yellowstone's loveliest scenes. Those who hike a half mile to the foot of the falls are richly rewarded. Tower Creek has been unable to keep pace with rapid downcutting of the larger Yellowstone River. Through a hanging canyon laced with rapids and

lined with spires, water races toward a 132-foot plunge to the bottom of Yellowstone's Grand Canyon. A cottony blanket of spray envelops the fall's base. Midday sun, illuminating deep recesses of the grotto-like canyon which embraces Tower Fall, creates a brilliant double rainbow.

At the lip of Tower Fall, a large boulder seemed to need merely a small push before it crashed to the rubble pile below. When the Washburn, Langford, and Doane expedition camped near the falls on August 27, 1870, the men placed bets on whether the boulder would be swept over the falls that night. Finally, the spring floods of 1986 toppled it from its precarious position.

Rapid downcutting by the Yellowstone River has left other waterfalls tucked along the canyon's walls. Hidden between the famous Upper and Lower Falls, Cascade Creek tumbles 129 feet over Crystal Falls. The water drops in three pitches initiated by a fern-lined sunken hollow. Because Crystal Falls is overshadowed by thundering

The Yellowstone Plateau's varied topography creates many spectacular waterfalls. Dropping toward Mammoth Hot Springs, Glen Creek breaks into stairsteps cascading over Rustic Falls (below). Deep within the backcountry, two forks of Mountain Ash Creek combine in 250-foot Union Falls (right). Hidden within Cascade Corner are at least fifty other waterfalls. Many are so seldom visited, they have never been named.

neighbors, visitors seldom see it. Its sequestered location is a peaceful interlude from the crowds frequenting the canyon rim.

Farther downstream, Surface Creek drains Ribbon Lake before entering the Grand Canyon northeast of Point Sublime. Many boulders cut the creek into white interlacing ribbons during its 1,000 foot dive to the river. Silver Cord Cascade is Yellowstone's longest perenial cascade. Across the park from the Grand Canyon, the Firehole River drops over three waterfalls. Thermal water, contributed by the Upper, Midway, and Lower Geyser basins, warms the river to 80°F during the summer. On frosty autumn mornings, gossamer strands of condensing steam enshroud the Cascades of the Firehole and Firehole falls.

A short hike from Biscuit Basin, the Little Firehole River departs the Madison Plateau when it drops eighty-five feet over Mystic Falls. Several fumaroles and seeping hot springs grace the canyon walls. Rising steam, glistening black volcanic rock, and lichen-draped spruce and firs give an eerie feeling to this graceful, curving cataract. During winter, the canyon below Mystic Falls becomes a fairyland of snow sculptures. Alice in Wonderland toadstools crown boulders. Splashing warm water chisels a stem from the snow capping each rock. Snow accumulating above the splash zone spreads into a toadstool cap. Snow adhering to tiny ledges on nearly vertical cliffs droops until an entire rock face is covered with smiling and frowning characters.

Three miles north of Mystic Falls, Fairy Creek's cold water reaches a notch in the Madison Plateau then plunges 197 feet. Prior to 1989, a beautiful clear pool graced the bottom of the falls. The North Fork Fire of 1988 partially burned the log jam forming a natural dam for the pool. Heavy rains in August of 1989 then washed away what remained of the dam, and the pool drained.

North-facing Fairy Falls remains shadowed from the sun's warming rays. Frigid temperatures cloak the waterfall in veils of long blue icicles. Fine spray freezing on nearby rock creates a mottled ice ball frosting. Extended cold snaps entomb the lower half of Fairy Falls in glistening ice.

Whether one considers the thundering Lower Falls or 300-foot-wide Cave Falls, each of Yellowstone's cataracts possesses special attributes. An observer once noted, "Yellowstone waterfalls complement the thermal activity perfectly. They are just geysers in reverse!"

66 Stay on this good fire-mountain
and spend the night among the stars.
Watch their glorious bloom until
the dawn, and get one more baptism
of light . . . you will remember these
fine, wild views, and look back with joy
to your wanderings in the blessed
old Yellowstone. **99**

John Muir
1901

For eleven miles a foot-worn trail winds along a rushing mountain stream and climbs through dense fallen trees. After crossing open meadows, the trail ends at Yellowstone's highest summer residence—the Mount Holmes fire lookout perched 10,336 feet above sea level. The fifteen and one-half foot square glass windowed house affords a commanding view over thousands of dark green lodgepole pines interspersed with green meadows and azure lakes. From this lofty summit, the immense area embraced by Yellowstone can be fully appreciated.

Mount Holmes is one of three fire lookouts staffed during the summer fire season. Fire lookout personnel traditionally were brought up the mountain by pack train. Today, instead of a difficult day-long journey with horses and mules, a helicopter makes the trip in fifteen to twenty minutes. When the lookout arrives in late June, snow on the saddle between Mount Holmes and nearby Dome Peak is often six to ten feet deep. Fifteen hundred feet below the summit, the upper Trilobite Lakes may be locked in ice well into July.

One Fourth of July, we were delivering mail and books to the Mount Holmes lookout. Twelve hundred feet below the summit a snowstorm struck. Icy clouds and swirling white flakes quickly enveloped us in a whiteout. Snow accumulated one to two inches per hour. We had a snowball fight followed by a lively discussion on whether this storm was the previous winter's last snow or the coming winter's first snow. After determining conditions were unsafe for further ascent, we trudged home. The mail could wait for calmer weather.

Savage weather is commonplace above tree line on Yellowstone's peaks. Three days after newlyweds Don and Nancy Hughes began duty as fire lookouts on Mount Holmes, they were welcomed by a tremendous windstorm. All day southwesterly winds howled across the peak. By late afternoon, rattling windows and whining guy wires drowned all but the loudest shouting. The last time the wind speed indicator was checked, it registered eighty to one hundred miles per hour. Soon afterward the anemometer's cups were blown off, the supporting pole bent in two, and finally the instrument was torn completely off its base.

During the night, the outhouse, which has one of the prettiest views of any Yellowstone privy, lost its roof to the formidable winds. A few weeks later, I found the roof's shattered remains a mile away among the Trilobite Lakes. Many summers earlier, before the little out-building was securely tethered, a lookout was taking his afternoon constitutional when strong winds tipped over the outhouse.

A month following the howling winds, Don and Nancy were treated to a wild electric storm considerably more severe than the typical afternoon thundershower. From Norris, I could see Mount Holmes illuminated almost continually by lightning. Bolts struck the ground at a rate of one per second. Outside the Mount Holmes lookout, the newly replaced anemometer glowed a brilliant blue. Nancy suggested they wear sunglasses to reduce the glare from lightning, guy wires, and anemometer. Inside the glass house, metal objects crackled, hissed, and snapped as charges built between mountain and cloud. The couple sat perched on well insulated cotton mattresses. Their feet were on a wooden stool with legs made

of glass insulators. As each charge grew, they braced themselves for the upcoming lightning flash and thunder explosion.

While Mount Holmes was deluged with hail and rain, Doug Haacke, the fire lookout twenty miles farther east on Mount Washburn, excitedly watched the approaching storm front. Lightning bolts instantaneously transformed Englemann spruce and subalpine fir into torches. Normally lookout personnel chart where strikes hit, so the area can be watched later for fires. So many trees

Pink blossoms of shooting star surround elk antlers (below) discarded in an alpine meadow. In early spring when bulls lose their antlers, mountain ridges are often blown snow-free, attracting hungry elk. Blackened skeletons of lodgepole pines (right) create stark contrast with winter's snow. Fire is a natural process in Yellowstone. Vigorous new growth will gradually reclaim forests burned during the fire season of 1988.

were rapidly struck, however, that it was impossible to keep track of the activity. Heavy rains following the lightning barrage extinguished most of the newly ignited fires. A few old snags remained quietly smoldering, waiting for an extended dry spell with warm winds to fan the embers back to life.

Unprotected hikers caught on Yellowstone's peaks by quickly growing thunderstorms have had harrowing experiences. Electric Peak, the Gallatin

Steaming ground at Norris melts winter's snow (left). Eleven miles beyond, the pyramid shaped peak of Mount Holmes shines brightly. Mount Holmes at the southern end of the Gallatin Range was uplifted by severe faulting and crumpling. Autumn turns Hayden Valley golden brown (above). With each storm's passing, the snow line on Mount Washburn lowers until Hayden Valley becomes engulfed in white. Mount Washburn is the eroding remnant of a 50 to 55 million-year-old volcano.

Range's highest mountain at 10,992 feet, looms over the northwest corner of Yellowstone. Its name implies a reputation for odd electrical phenomena experienced by many who climb its craggy summit.

One summer afternoon, two friends reached the summit of Electric Peak just as a dark cumulonimbus cloud approached. Suddenly a tingling sensation rippled through their skin. The men were aware that their normally flat hair was rising into a wildly moving vertical style. They began laughing and taking pictures, but soon came to a frightening realization—the mountain's positive charge was building toward a lightning strike. With crackling hair and sparks flashing from their heels, they made a hasty descent from danger.

Extremely harsh weather occurring at Yellowstone's higher elevations causes timberline to range between 9,000 and 10,000 feet. Above tree line, alpine plants hug the ground avoiding dessication from biting winds. As the snow line recedes through June and July, moss campion, alpine forget-me-not, sky pilot, and many other small blossoms carpet mountains between lichen-covered boulders. Even on the windiest days during the short blooming season, a fragrant aroma envelopes alpine plant

communities. Insect pollinators need pungent olfactory clues to locate alpine flowers in a raw, windy environment.

Bird life is sparse in Yellowstone's rugged high country. Shunning the protective cover of lower elevations, gray-crowned rosy finches and Sprague's pipits nest in rocky tundra. Pipits and rosy finches share their lofty expanse with golden eagles, prairie falcons, and ravens who seek the mountain's strong updrafts.

Bighorn sheep also utilize the alpine meadow forage. An estimated 250 to 400 rams, ewes and lambs traverse the high country each summer. When feeding, continual movement keeps each flock from overgrazing sparse tundra vegetation. Circular hooves with a rock-grabbing depression seemingly glue the bighorns to precarious ledges and steep slopes. Sheep avoid predators and find forage not utilized by other herbivores by traversing these cliffs. The three-mile hike up Mount Washburn is excellent for viewing bighorn ewes with their lambs and occasionally, magnificently curled horned rams. Protected from hunting pressure, Mount Washburn's bighorns are nonchalant about human presence. Hikers resting in Washburn's meadows are often surrounded by grazing bighorns.

Yellowstone's rocky slopes provide homes for pikas or conies. These tiny members of the rabbit family announce their presence with a plaintive "beeen" call. Because pikas are more wary than the bighorns, one must remain motionless and silent to observe them going about their summer chores of picking cony hay. This small rabbit gathers a mouthful of vegetation, then scurries between talus boulders to cache its food in an underground chamber. Since the pika's forage is often blossoming, these elf-like creatures often appear to be collecting flower bouquets. When winter turns the talus slope surface into an inhospitable environment, an underground storehouse awaits to fuel each pika.

Also sharing rocky high country exposures is the yellow-bellied marmot, a rather fat relative of the woodchuck found in the eastern states. Marmots often lie spread-eagle atop large boulders sunning themselves. Rather than industriously gathering and drying food for winter consumption, marmots acquire a thick rolling fat supply metabolized during an eight month hibernation.

Moving below timberline, the biomass

Morning fog lifting from Swan Lake Flats reveals the 10,992-foot summit of Electric Peak (left). Part of the Gallatin Range, Electric Peak was for many years considered Yellowstone's highest point. More thorough surveying revealed many peaks in the Absaroka Range were higher, with 11,358-foot Eagle Peak crowning all park mountains. Approximately eighty percent of park forests are lodgepole pine. Lack of sunlight beneath lodgepoles often limits the ground cover to mosses and lichens (above).

increases dramatically. The diversity of plant species found across Yellowstone is low for a region with such varied amounts of precipitation. Approximately eleven inches of precipitation occur annually near Gardiner, Montana, while seventy to eighty inches fall near the continental divide in southern Yellowstone. Just thirteen species of trees, eight of them conifers, are found within the park. There are slightly more than 1,100 species of flowering plants.

Recently glaciation, scouring all but the tops of Yellowstone's highest peaks, almost swept the region clean of vegetation. Between periods of ice entombment, vast rhyolitic lava flows and volcanic ash fallout repeatedly retarded vegetation establishment. When conditions finally became suitable for forest regrowth, only those species close to the Yellowstone plateau reclaimed barren ground.

Seventy-seven percent of Yellowstone's timber is lodgepole, leading some casual observers incorrectly to believe it is the park's only species. Where twenty to forty inches of precipitation fall annually, lodgepoles thrive on nutritionally poor soils derived from rhyolite. Their slow growth rate causes trees older than 300 years to have diameters of only twelve to twenty inches. Forest fires are the key to lodgepole pine success. The trees bear two types of cones, those which open under normal conditions to disperse seeds and those called serotinous which remain tightly closed until a fire heats them to 140°F. Following a fire, seedling lodgepoles establish ground cover and begin a new cycle.

For thousands of years, lightning-caused fires have been an integral part of the Yellowstone ecosystem. Suppressing lightning fires is contrary to the goal of maintaining completely natural working systems within the park.

Early management in Yellowstone thought otherwise. Just as wolves and mountain lions were labeled "bad" and targeted for extermination, fires were considered "bad" and suppressed whenever possible.

With time came enlightenment. In 1972, a natural prescribed fire policy was initiated. Every fire was assessed to determine whether it would be allowed to burn or be suppressed. Fires caused by humans and natural fires moving toward developed areas were extinguished immediately if possible. In addition, fires which might spread to adjacent lands not managed by similar fire policies were fought. Natural fires not threatening human life or development were allowed to burn until extinguished naturally by heavy precipitation or exhaustion of fuel.

During the sixteen-year period from 1972 through 1987, tens of thousands of lightning strikes resulted in 235 fires in Yellowstone National Park and adjacent lands. The average size for naturally ignited fires burning to extinction was a mere 250 acres. The largest single burn encompassed 7,400 acres. Prevailing opinion was that, except for the oldest stands of lodgepole pine mixed with Engelmann spruce and subalpine fir, Yellowstone's forests were relatively nonflammable.

Then came the fire season of 1988. Several years of below average annual precipitation culminated with 1988 being the driest year since records were established in 1886. By mid-summer, fuel moisture in Yellowstone's green forests was less than that of kiln-dried lumber. Numerous lightning strikes occurred in June and July without the benefit of fire-quenching rains. In August, six dry cold-fronts passed through the park, packing extreme winds.

Much of Yellowstone was already prime for a major conflagration. Before

A bighorn ewe (below) gazes from the slopes of Mount Washburn to the Gallatin Range on the horizon. Sure footed bighorns feed in the rugged mountains where competition from other herbivores is less. A phlox (right) copes with harsh conditions on top of Mount Washburn by blooming in a crack between lichen covered boulders. In such small niches, plants avoid desiccating winds and perhaps the teeth of a hungry sheep.

the 1988 fires, approximately one-third of the park's forests were 250 to 350 years old. In many stands that age, Engelmann spruce and subalpine fir had invaded the forest floor and grown into the canopy. Unlike lodgepole pines, which shed branches during growth, spruce and fir retain their highly flammable lower branches. Dead lodgepole pines in old growth forests add to the fuel load.

Many cycles in Nature span time periods much longer than a human life. And so it is with Yellowstone's fire cycle. Perhaps every 250 to 400 years, when conditions become dry enough, Yellowstone experiences major fire seasons similar to the summer of 1988. Data from coring old-growth lodgepole pines reveals periods of substantial fires

Climax forests destined to burn and exceedingly dry conditions triggered the fires of 1988 (photo to left by Jennifer Whipple). Approximately 793,880 acres, or 36 percent of the park, burned. Lightning strikes in June and July (above) ignited some of the blazes, while other fires were human caused. Individual trees smoldered and burned into November (photo to right by Jennifer Whipple), when winter's snow finally extinguished all flames. Fires begin new cycles of forest regrowth vital for healthy wildlife.

between 1690 and 1710 a.d. and again from 1730 to 1750 a.d.

For decades following these large burns, most of Yellowstone's forests comprised a mosaic of early and middle successional stages that, except in the driest of years, was relatively inflammable. But by 1930, most of these stands had aged sufficiently to become a tinderbox waiting for ignition. It was inevitable that, eventually, a large portion of the park would burn again.

The extreme drought of 1988 set the stage for both lightning and human caused fires to roar across the landscape. Driven by winds up to 70 miles per hour, the flames readily consumed even young stands of lodgepole pine. The 25,000 firefighters and 120 million dollars thrown at the fires did little more than protect developed areas within the park and surrounding towns. Nature held the upper hand.

The sound of a firestorm is absolutely awe inspiring. Approaching Old Faithful on September 9, 1988, the second firestorm in three days created a colossal roar, like a hundred freight trains barreling down Iron Creek. Thick, pungent smoke obscured the rolling wall of flame. Firebrands were carried aloft to ignite spot fires as much as two miles ahead of the storm.

After the fire storm passed, calm returned. The hills surrounding Old Faithful sparkled as if lighted by a thousand twinkling campfires. Snags burned through their trunks and crashed to the ground. Bison bulls grunted and roared in late summer rut. Geysers erupted. Hot Springs gurgled. Normalcy was returning to the park.

All told, an estimated 793,880 acres or 36 percent of Yellowstone burned in 1988. Initial reports and sensationalism by public media indicated considerably larger figures. Much of the fire pattern was spotty, leaving the charred forests interspersed with islands and peninsulas of living trees. The newly-created forest edges will provide diversity of habitat for decades to come. Fireweed, aspen and seedling lodgepole pines will reclaim the land. Mice and elk will find fresh browse.

Yellowstone was altered not for the worse, not for the better, but as part of the dynamic system of natural change and diversity that is vital to a healthy ecosystem.

Without fires, the lodgepole pine's susceptibility to insect attack increases. When the trees become eight to twelve inches in diameter, their attractiveness to mountain pine bark beetles rises. Heavy infestations mottle the forest with orange-brown dying trees. The beetles tend to kill older trees, opening the canopy to young lodgepoles and forest floor plants. An uneven aged lodgepole stand results, which provides more food for elk and deer. Additional windfall furnishes fuel for future fires that in turn start the reforestation cycle.

A single female bark beetle never would stand a chance of exterminating a lodgepole pine. While she can burrow beneath the bark and lay her eggs, a healthy tree's heavy resin flow would paralyze her larvae's attempt to consume the cambium, the living portion of the tree. Females excrete minute quantities of powerful chemical that lures not only male bark beetles for mating, but also attracts other females. The beetles mount an attack which overwhelms the tree's resistance. They also introduce a fungus that further weakens a lodgepole. Orange needles and a trunk peppered with tiny holes exuding milky sap laced with sawdust mark an old ldogepole's demise.

In the northern parts of Yellowstone, Douglas firs are periodically seized by another insect infestation, the western spruce budworm. Before developing into light brown moths, small caterpillars consume new fir needles. Heavy outbreaks lasting for many summers kill most young Douglas firs and cause older trees to lose their crowns. Infestations of mountain pine bark beetles and western spruce budworms have occurred for thousands of years. The two tree-killing insect species are as important to the Yellowstone ecosystem as are elk and grizzly bears. Within the park, therefore, outbreaks are allowed to run their course. Yellowstone's naturally working system remains intact for people to watch but not to manipulate.

Growing above 7,000 feet is an additional conifer, the whitebark pine, whose distribution constitutes a real curiosity. Whitebark pine are often found in narrow strips on the leeward side of ridges. Additionally, individual whitebarks may be discovered tucked in lodgepole forets miles from a seed source. Rather than finding an individual tree, one usually encounters many whitebark trunks growing together. This suggests two possibilities. Either the trees are stump sprouts resulting from logging operations or the trunks represent successful progeny from a cached seed supply. Since commercial timber harvesting has not been allowed in Yellowstone, the second possibility is most probable. Yet what seed-caching animal would hide its booty miles from a parent-tree source?

Dr. Steve Vander Wall of Utah State University, while performing research in Yellowstone and other western localities, discovered that the seed dispersing animal was not generally a rodent but a bird, the Clark's nutcracker. During late summer this large raucous relative of jays and crows gathers enormous quantities of whitebark pine nuts. Each mouthful of nuts is flown to a variety of caching sites. Wind swept slopes that are blown snow-free, fissures in cliffs, and the walls of Yellowstone's Grand Canyon are favorite locations for storing pine nuts utilized during winter. Wooded areas and locations that hold snow may be used to safely store seeds recovered during the spring and early summer.

Dr. Vander Wall found that Clark's nutcrackers locate buried seed caches by memory. An individual bird may dig thousands of caches annually. Seeds not recovered, if planted in the proper environment, can grow into mature whitebark pines.

Below treeline, whitebark pine seeds have slim chances for survival when planted within sloping mountainside meadows. Desiccating winds, tree snapping avalanches, and fires maintain mountain meadows by limiting conifer encroachment.

At lower elevations, expansive treeless areas like Hayden Valley, Pelican Valley, and Gibbon Meadow occupy former lake bottoms. Glacial ice or lava flows impounding water created these ancient lakes. Thick lake bottom sediments seem to preclude tree establishment. Horn and antler rubbing activities by bison and elk, fires, and poorly drained soils further discourage seedling trees in grassland and sagebrush areas.

Yellowstone's lowest elevations near Gardiner, Montana, receive only eleven inches of annual precipitation. In the shadow of towering Electric Peak, which looms a mile above the Yellowstone River, plants typical of the northern Great Basin Desert survive. Saltbrush, greasewood, and prickly pear cactus thrive in this dry valley blocked from moisture by the nearby Gallatin Range.

For miles, Yellowstone offers a pristine expanse of unfenced meadows, forests, and alpine tundra similar to a time when the only human touches were the impressions of moccasins. Perhaps Yellowstone's greatest value is that it provides the opportunity to learn that a natural system of checks and balances, including forest fires, insect infestations, and winter starvation, can maintain an ecosystem without human manipulation.

"The lake lay before us, a vast sheet of
quiet water, of a most delicate
ultramarine hue, one of the most
beautiful scenes I have ever beheld…
The great object of all our labors had
been reached and we were amply
paid for all our toils. Such a vision is worth a
lifetime, and only one of such marvelous
beauty will ever greet human eyes.**"**

Ferdinand V. Hayden
1872

The world's largest collection of geysers, native herds of large roaming mammals, thundering waterfalls, and spectacular canyons qualifies Yellowstone as four national parks, not one. The park also contains more than 200 sparkling blue lakes. From tiny Isa Lake straddling the continental divide to 136 square mile Yellowstone Lake, each body of water is a jewel enhancing Yellowstone's beauty.

At an elevation of 7,733 feet, Yellowstone Lake is North America's largest body of water at such a high elevation. Although park roads follow its perimeter for twenty-nine miles, most of Yellowstone Lake's more than 100 miles of shoreline are ruggedly wild. Ragged peaks of the Absaroka Mountains, backdropping the east shore, reflect serenely when the lake calms to a mirror finish. Mount Sheridan, Flat Mountain, Chicken Ridge, and the Promontory add topography to the southwest. The lake's southern portions are divided into three narrow inlets. Long beaches of black volcanic sand are interspersed with inpenetrable tangles of wind-fallen spruce, fir, and lodgepole pine.

Yellowstone Lake has many contrasting moods. The transition from lapping blue water to white ice is a fascinating yearly change. Events heralding the eventual metamorphosis begin in late August when water heated during warm summer days encounters cold night air funneling down valleys onto the lake. Like a gigantic cup of cooling coffee, condensing water vapor covers the lake in morning mist. Following particularly cold moist nights, thick fog envelops the lake until midmorning.

The wail of a common loon and the piercing cry of a California gull drift across foggy, still waters. Pattering of wings and webbed feet disclose a hidden family of common mergansers taking flight. In a few months, the lake will freeze. Its birds depart for warmer climates or open stretches on the Yellowstone River.

The first signs of freezing occur across many shallow lakeside lagoons hemmed by sandy beaches. During chilly October nights, a skim of ice creeps across each pool. Each night's quiet efforts are broken by warm rays of the morning sun teaming with gusty winds. Eventually the ponds become ice locked for seven months.

Before the lake freezes, November gales whip its water into frenzied motion. Snow squalls reduce visibility to a few hundred feet. Dark gray water with thousands of whitecaps blends into an equally gray sky. Winds bite with an icy cold. Waves crash against shoreline rocks and fallen trees. When the winds abate and the sky clears, glistening ice coats all wave-splashed objects. Trees wear crystalline blue skirts, and boulders glisten like the sparkling interior of a quartz geode.

The lake freezes much later than the shallow lagoons. When water cools to 39° F, it sinks and is replaced by warmer water rising from below. With an average depth of 139 feet, a long time is required for the entire lake to reach a homogeneous 39° F.

The lake's transformation occurs on an intensely cold night. The thermometer can plunge below zero in late October, to 30° F below zero in November, and toward the park's record cold of 66° F below zero during December and January. A few weeks prior to this, protected bays freeze. Should a storm develop during the freezing process, thin ice shatters like a huge pane of glass being smashed against the earth. Waves stack the broken pieces into a sturdy shoreline fortress that may stretch for miles.

At night stars shine brilliantly through Yellowstone's crystal clear air. Gently lapping water reflects the sky's image. The offshore breeze is frigid. Ripples encountering growing ice produce a tinsel melody. During the early morning, the surface freezes. When the rising sun clears the Absaroka Mountains and shines across the solid expanse, an incredible event happens.

On a 20° F below zero January morning when freeze-up seemed likely, I traveled to West Thumb. I stopped at Duck Lake to watch fog lift from the West Thumb Geyser Basin along Yellowstone Lake's

A flock of California gulls (below) fly across the calm water of Yellowstone Lake near Wolf Point. White pelicans, double-crested cormorants, and Caspian terns nest with the gulls on two tiny islands in the Southeast Arm. Most of Yellowstone Lake's shoreline is rough, rocky wilderness (right). Waves roll ashore near appropriately named Rock Point as the sky clouds over before a storm.

west shore a half mile away. A bellowing moan came from the plain of ice carpeting West Thumb. Overnight the lake had frozen. The music of the lake serenaded me. I hurried to the West Thumb shore to listen to the morning symphony. As the sun warmed new

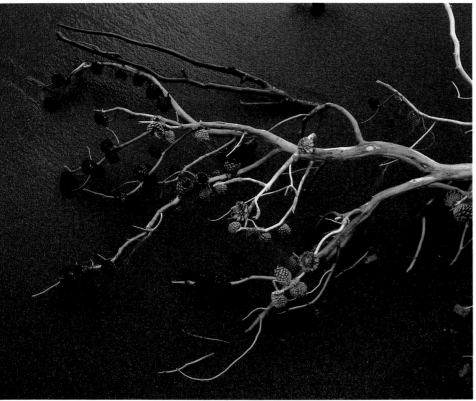

Volcanic sand carried by storm tossed waves abrades trees that have fallen into Yellowstone Lake. The driftwood becomes polished bronze and silver gems resting upon beds of black velvet. An old stump partially buried in the sand (left) weathers into gnarled beauty. Waves stripped the bark from a lodgepole pine (above) but left the cones attached to gleaming silver wood.

ice, the lake responded noisily. Creaks, groans, booms, zings, sputters, gurgles, yelps, and wails echoed off the forested shore. The music rose and fell in pitch and intensity. Clouds casting shadows on the ice turned the music on and off with their passing.

Solar radiation heating and expanding the thin ice sheet created the concert. An unfrozen stretch of water remained close to the West Thumb Hot Springs. Ice expansion generated strings of waves rippling across still water. As the day warmed, edges of the ice sheet pushed onshore. Sections buckled, building triangular tunnels upon the ice surface and thrusting slabs on top of one another. I was witnessing a natural model of mountain building.

Readings from a seismograph installed along the southern part of Yellowstone Lake puzzled scientists from the United States Geological Survey. Each winter the instrument recorded an intense swarm of activity. The source remained a mystery until finally it was realized that vibrations from ice expanding and contracting were being transmitted to the bedrock.

Snowstorms occur every few days during most winters. A thick blanket insulating the ice from warming and cooling silences the lake's singing. During the first winter I heard the music of the lake, snow did not fall for two weeks following freeze-up. When conditions allowed safe ice travel, beautiful abstract scenery awaited. Beneath five to eight inches of clear ice, redside shiners, a species of minnow, were visible swimming along the rocky bottom. Gas bubbles rising from the lake bottom became amoeba-like figures embedded in gray ice. Cracks conveying moist air were lined with a two to four-inch fleece of frost. When a breeze arose, frost clusters cleaved from their bases and scurried across the ice like diminutive armies. White powder trails marked their passage until each was obliterated. Snowfall finally veiled the lake. Except for an occasional baritone rumble as ice settled beneath heavy snow, the lake's music ceased.

During twenty-five years of observation, Lake winterkeeper Jerry Bateson saw the earliest freeze-up occur on December 10. The latest happened on January 16. December 25, Christmas Day, was the average date for freezing over. Most of the park remains snowbound for seven to eight months. Yellowstone Lake wears its winter wrap for an average of 182 days—half the year. When deep snowfall accumulates immediately following freeze-up, the insulating blanket greatly retards ice thickening. The lake then becomes dangerous for travel.

The ice disappears between May 16 and June 11. The warm spring sun melts snow capping the lake. For a brief period, the surface is a storybook. Animal tracks buried for months within the snow blanket reappear. One spot shows tracks where a snowshoe hare ventured into the ice hundreds of feet from protective cover. Perhaps the hare was lured onto the great white expanse to perform its mid-winter mating dance. In another area scores of coyote tracks converge upon a patch of snow discolored by bits of hair. Here is evidence that an unwary muskrat was killed. Similar stories appear for miles along the shore. The pages are erased when soft snow becomes melt water.

As break-up approaches, the ice retains most of its thickness but structurally weakens. If one attempted to walk on its honeycombed surface, the ice would shatter into hundreds of slender needles. When the ice finally goes out, it vanishes quickly. Blue water returns

79

Warm light of late afternoon does little to stop the chill of a November wind blowing across West Thumb. Snowmelt brings the lake to its highest water level during early summer. Storms which can whip the high water into six-foot waves gnaw away the shoreline, leaving a fortress of fallen trees.

where only a few hours before there was ice.

Yellowstone Lake's tranquil appearance contrasts with the volcanic fury that excavated its basin. North of the South and Southeast Arms, the lake occupies a portion of the twenty-eight by forty-seven mile volcanic crater forged from the Yellowstone Plateau 600,000 years ago. Originally the entire crater contained a much larger lake. Subsequent volcanic eruptions built ridges and plateaus that fragmented the body of water. Shoshone and Lewis lakes are remnants that still drain to the Pacific through the Snake River system. Volcanic flows cut Yellowstone Lake from its western drainage. Now its waters flow north through the Yellowstone River toward the Mississippi River and the Gulf of Mexico.

Between 125,000 and 200,000 years ago, a volcanic eruption and subsequent collapse created a four by six-mile crater located within the major explosion caldera. The blast was a small version of the event that happened 600,000 years ago. West Thumb occupies the smaller oval depression. Its dimensions are similar to a more famous caldera, Crater Lake in Oregon.

Glaciation further assisted in carving Yellowstone Lake. At least three times ice buried the lake. During the recent Pinedale glacial period, approximately 15,000 years ago, ice capping the lake thickened to 3,000 feet. Its mass grew high enough to spawn its own snowfall and flow across most of the park. When the Pinedale glaciers retreated, water was suddenly released, rapidly draining lakes trapped behind the ice. In many locations pockets of superheated water were trapped beneath the lakes. Draining caused a swift release of pressure, allowing superheated water to flash into steam. It was as if a giant hand had removed the lid from a colossal pressure cooker. Huge explosions blasted craters in the lake beds, and debris flew thousands of feet.

Wasting of the Pinedale ice caused an extraordinarily rapid 200-foot drop in Yellowstone Lake's level. One or more explosions, triggered by the lowering

water, created a mile long crater with a maximum depth of 160 feet. Mary Bay on Yellowstone Lake's north shore surrounds the oval depression. On the north and east sides of Mary Bay expelled material formed a curved ridge 200 feet high, one-half to one and one-half miles wide and three miles long.

Between 3,500 and 5,500 years ago, an approximate ten-foot lowering in lake level sufficiently released pressure to blast a crater now holding Indian Pond north of Mary Bay. Turbid and Fern lakes are other depressions forged by hydrothermal explosions occurring at different times.

Beneath Yellowstone Lake, pockets of superheated water await future lake level reductions. A particularly hot spot is near Stevenson Island. When geologist Dr. Robert Smith's research crew embedded a probe sixteen feet into the mucky bottom, sediment samples brought to the surface were too hot to touch. Temperatures well in excess of

the surface boiling point were recorded twelve feet beneath the lake bottom. If another water level drop occurs, Yellowstone Lake could repeat geologic history with additional hydrothermal explosions.

In addition to its fascinating geology, Yellowstone Lake offers much for wildlife observers and anglers. The lake teams with native cutthroat trout, named for the bright red stripes that slash across their throat. The cutthroat is normally indigenous to waters draining to the Pacific. At one time Yellowstone Lake emptied into the Pacific and cutthroat may have entered then. Another possibility is that Snake River cutthroat swam across a shallow marshy area atop Two Ocean Pass. Here water flows freely north to the Atlantic and south to the

Yellowstone Lake freezes each year within a few weeks of Christmas. Cracks rifle through the surface as the new ice contracts and expands (left), producing an unearthly music of groans and chatters. Thickening ice traps gas (above right) vented from the lake bottom near the West Thumb Geyser Basin. A blanket of snow soon silences the lake's music and hides the ice patterns.

Pacific. Through much of their range, cutthroats have hybridized with rainbow trout introduced from the west coast. In Yellowstone Lake, the bloodline remains pure.

Fish watching is a popular park activity. Below Fishing Bridge at Yellowstone Lake's northern outlet, scores of sixteen to eighteen-inch cutthroat swim in emerald green water. For many years, the bridge was shoulder to shoulder with fishermen. Intense fishing disrupted spawning cutthroats. The activity was contrary to Yellowstone's enabling legislation forbidding the "wanton destruction of wildlife."

Attempting a return to natural conditions, park management banned fishing from Fishing Bridge in 1973. In addition, spawning waters were closed and restrictive catch limits imposed. Anglers may now enjoy catching and releasing large cutthroats in other park locations.

Reduced fishing was important not only for maintaining a healthy cutthroat population but also for feeding an assortment of birds and mammals. In May and June when cutthroats spawn up Yellowstone Lake's tributaries, grizzly bears patrol the creeks. The person who discovers the grizzly's distinctive two rutted trail paralleling a creek should be wary. This four-legged fisherman is quite protective of its catch.

White pelicans feed primarily on mature cutthroat trout. Molly Islands in Yellowstone Lake's Southeast Arm support a healthy white pelican population during the summer nesting season. Many people are surprised to see pelicans living inland. Unlike their brown coastal cousins, white pelicans establish nesting colonies on large western fresh water lakes. One prerequisite for pelicans is isolation. People are not allowed within a quarter mile of the Molly Islands, and boating is restricted to hand-propelled craft. Here pelicans find the seclusion they require.

Hundreds of California gulls and smaller numbers of Caspian terns and double-crested cormorants share the Molly Islands. During successful breeding seasons, more than 2,000 birds utilize the two islands barely totaling an acre.

Approximately thirty-five pairs of ospreys nest along the lake perimeter and on Frank Island. Osprey fly above the lake's deep water, whose surface is frequented by young cutthroats. When a fish is spotted, the osprey dives. One study in the park showed that ospreys successfully captured fish during forty-

seven percent of their dives. Ninety-three percent of the diet of Yellowstone Lake Ospreys was cutthroat trout.

Late one winter I was amused by the antics of otters catching cutthroats near Steamboat Point. Three otters were using holes melted through the ice by underwater hot springs. One otter would dive beneath the ice, capture a trout, then resurface to consume its meal. Nearby were eight coyotes well versed in otter fishing habits. The moment an otter appeared with a trout, there was mass commotion. Coyotes, who moments before were sulking in the sun, galloped toward the otter.

Realizing its meal was about to be stolen, the otter would dive with its fish. The coyotes skidded to a halt beside the empty hole. With keen eyes, they surveyed the surrounding holes and waited. When the otter appeared, the mêlée repeated. While the coyotes were charging, the otter hastily gobbled its fish. When the coyotes arrived, the otter attempted to continue feeding by taking the fish to the pool's opposite side. A few additional bites were swallowed before the coyotes raced around the pool's perimeter. With much snarling and bickering, the coyotes eventually pilfered the fish.

Time after time, coyotes successfully

stole fish. Between episodes, otters and coyotes peacefully sunned next to each other. One might wonder why the larger coyotes did not capture an otter for dinner. They seemed to understand that eating otters would end their freeloading. A substantial portion of Yellowstone's predators would disappear if the cutthroat population were reduced by human over-fishing.

Much of Yellowstone's aquatic system is not in pristine condition. For thousands of years, natural barriers kept many park streams barren of trout. Early park managers sought to "improve" these waters by introducing not only

September morning mist silhouettes the sandy spit of Wolf Point (below). Mist forms during nights that are considerably cooler than the lake's temperature. A steaming lake signals summer's ending. For half the year Yellowstone Lake is locked in ice. A hot spring reflects the sun at West Thumb Geyser Basin (right). Thermal water keeps only a small portion of West Thumb from freezing.

cutthroat but also alien trout species. Brown trout were brought from Europe. Rainbow trout came from the West Coast. Brook trout were secured from eastern United States and Canada. Lake trout arrived from the Great Lakes. In many cases these exotics competed with and displaced the eleven fish species and one hybrid naturally occurring in Yellowstone.

The Madison, Firehole, and Gibbon

Thousands of frost rosettes cover new lake ice (left) following a calm, intensely cold night. On the sandy shore of Breeze Point strong winds prune branches, cones, and needles from a lodgepole pine.(right). The winds sculpt exposed shoreline trees. The bright yellow-green growth is wolf lichen, while the darker lichen is known as old man's beard.

Rivers were stocked with rainbow and brook trout. Downstream from Kepler Cascades and Gibbon Falls, the now rare Arctic grayling was the only member of the salmon family originally present. Introduced trout have made the three rivers renowned fishing streams but at the expense of Arctic grayling. Grayling are now rarely found in their original waters. They are more common on Grebe, Wolf, Ice, and Cascade lakes where they were introduced during the 1920s and 1930s.

Plantings of other fish also occurred. Black bass, yellow perch, and land-locked salmon were introduced at various times. Fortunately none of these species remain in the park.

Fish hatcheries were constructed at Lake Village, Grebe Lake, and Trout Lake providing cutthroat and grayling stock for waters in the park and around the world. Between 1899 and 1956 hatchery personnel stripped 818 million eggs from female cutthroats attempting to spawn in Yellowstone Lake tributaries.

Creating even more disruption, bait fishermen inadvertently introduced longnose suckers, redside shiners, and lake chubs to Yellowstone Lake. Originally the lake contained two species of fish, cutthroat trout, and a type of minnow called the longnose dace. Five species now reside in the lake.

Present fisheries management calls for maintaining natural populations of native species. Alien fish are removed where feasible, and fishing is allowed when there is minimal disruption of natural populations. Regulations vary from year to year. The park requires anglers to obtain a free fishing permit that gives details about means and limits.

Tributaries feeding Yellowstone Lake come from the snow gracing pristine mountain meadows. From cascading creeks water enters one of North America's prettiest lakes. The water brings nutrients that support a vast biota from phytoplankton to ospreys. As it leaves Yellowstone Lake, the water courses through the wildlife rich Hayden Valley and tumbles into the magnificent Grand Canyon. Then it goes through a second chasm, the Black Canyon of the Yellowstone.

At Gardiner, Montana, the river leaves Yellowstone's sanctuary. It flows northeast across Montana to its confluence with the Missouri, a journey of 671 miles. The Yellowstone River is the only major river in the lower forty-eight states not dammed. Perhaps the river's pure beginnings carry downstream a message of preservation.

The river's free flowing nature tantalizes dam developers. Frequently there is talk of damming the Yellowstone north of the park and flooding Paradise Valley. Environmental consciousness has prevailed, and the river flows unrestrained.

Just as the Yellowstone River may eventually be harnessed, the park is not immune from modern society's encroachment. Geothermal drilling outside park borders could sap Yellowstone's geysers of energy needed for erupting. Nearby mineral and oil development may impair the park's wilderness character. Can Yellowstone survive the annual impact of 2½ million visitors? The conscience of America will dictate Yellowstone's future.

For the time being, ospreys dive into pure water capturing untainted trout. Grizzly bears stir up ant hills searching for a favorite food. People marvel at Old Faithful shooting a sparkling column of boiling water 130 feet high.

Even though mankind has absorbed Yellowstone's profound wonders and beauty for more than a century, the park remains in excellent condition. Yellowstone is a great natural oasis in a land mostly tailored to fulfill human needs. On March 1, 1872, Yellowstone was set aside "for the benefit and enjoyment of the people." We are fortunate that our forefathers preserved Yellowstone for future generations.

Acknowledgments

I am greatly indebted to many people who interrupted their schedules to assist me. Yellowstone Park geologist Rick Hutchinson and his naturalist wife, Jennifer, unselfishly shared their home, ignoring my 6 a.m. trips to greet sunrise in the geyser basin. Both friends were always willing to dig out obscure reports in Rick's "I can always find it" filing system. Mary Meagher, chief park research biologist, offered many helpful suggestions. Plant ecologist Don Despain gave excellent assistance during a time when 18,000 acres of Yellowstone were on fire. Alan Mebane, chief park naturalist, kindly reviewed the manuscript.

In researching obscure bits of information, Lee Whittlesey, who is striving to uncover the history of every Yellowstone place name, was invaluable. Tim Manns, park historian, helped locate fascinating, century-old documents in Yellowstone's archives. United States Geological Survey geologists Don White, Al Truesdell, Mitch Pitt, and Mike Thompson, as well as Bob Smith from the University of Utah, enthusiastically shared their theories on Yellowstone's underground workings. Gerald Richmond's report on the Grand Canyon of the Yellowstone provided many interesting facts. Steve Vander Wall taught me that Clark's nutcrackers are smarter than the average bird. Don and Nancy Hughes vividly described their summer on Mount Holmes.

For help in preparing draft manuscripts, I always will be grateful to Carol and John Borthwick, and to my parents, Fred and Tavie Hirschman. They spent countless hours poring over the text. Good friend Cheryl Bloethe was incredibly patient typing revision after revision. Her thoughtful suggestions on the text and photographs were invaluable. Many ideas and photographs came during warmly remembered backcountry trips with Steve Bogen, Doug Pfeiffer, Linda Henning, Frank and Judy Balthis, and Mike and Barb Pflaum.

To all who assisted with the book, my warmest thanks.

Sources of Quotations

Page 1
Raynolds, William F. *Brevet Brigadier General W. F. Raynolds on the Exploration of the Yellowstone and the Country Drained by That River.* (40th Congress, First Sess.; Senate Exec. Doc. 77.) Washington, D.C.: Government Printing Office, 1868.

Page 3
Hedges, Cornelius. "Yellowstone Lake." *Helena Daily Herald,* November 9, 1870.

Page 5
Hayden, Ferdinand Vandiveer. "The Wonders of the West—II: More About Yellowstone." *Scribner's Monthly,* February 1872.

Page 7
Hayden, Ferdinand Vandiveer. "The Wonders of the West—II: More About Yellowstone." *Scribner's Monthly,* February 1872.

Page 13
Hedges, Cornelius. "Hell-broth Springs." *Helena Daily Herald,* October 19, 1870.

Page 19
Langford, Nathaniel P. "The Ascent of Mount Hayden." *Scribner's Monthly,* June 1873.

Page 39
Roosevelt, Theodore. *Outdoor Pastimes of an American Hunter.* New York: Charles Scribner's Sons, 1923.

Page 51
Langford, Nathaniel P. "The Wonders of Yellowstone." *Scribner's Monthly,* May 1871.

Page 63
Muir, John. *Our National Parks.* Boston: Houghton Mifflin Co., 1901.

Page 75
Hayden, Ferdinand Vandiveer. *Preliminary Report of the United States Geological Survey of Montana and Portions of Adjacent Territories; Being a Fifth Annual Report of Progress.* Washington, D.C.: Government Printing Office, 1872.

Uncaptioned Photographs

Cover
Subzero winter eruption, Old Faithful.

Page 1
Ice on lodgepole pine. West Thumb Geyser Basin.

Pages 2 & 3
January eruption, Old Faithful.

Pages 4 & 5
Boardwalk, Norris Geyser Basin.

Pages 6 & 7
Lower Falls, Yellowstone River.

Pages 8 & 9
Bison, Hayden Valley.

Pages 10 & 11
Night view of the North Fork Fire, 1988.
(photo by Jennifer Whipple)

Page 13
Simultaneous eruptions, Beehive (foreground) and Old Faithful.

Page 19
Giantess Geyser, Upper Geyser Basin.

Page 39
Bull moose, Yellowstone River.

Page 51
Lower Falls, Yellowstone River.

Page 63
Meadow south of Yellowstone Lake.

Page 75
Dead trees, Yellowstone Lake.